THE
FAT
LADY
SANG

ALSO BY ROBERT EVANS

The Kid Stays in the Picture

THE
FAT
LADY
SANG

ROBERT
EVANS

*it***books**

AN IMPRINT OF HARPERCOLLINS PUBLISHERS

*it***books**

Article on pages 201–3 reprinted by permission of the *Wall Street Journal*, copyright © 2013 Dow Jones & Company, Inc. All rights reserved worldwide. License number 3222040489258.

Unless otherwise indicated, all photographs are courtesy of the author.

HarperCollins books may be purchased for educational, business, or sales promotional use. For information please e-mail the Special Markets Department at SPsales@harpercollins.com.

FIRST EDITION

Designed by Paula Russell Szafranski

Library of Congress Cataloging-in-Publication Data
Evans, Robert, 1930–
    The fat lady sang / Robert Evans. — First edition.
        p.   cm
    ISBN 978-0-06-228604-8 (pbk.)—ISBN 978-0-06-222834-5 (ebook) 1. Evans, Robert, 1930- —Health. 2. Cerebrovascular disease—Patients—Biography. 3. Motion picture producers and directors—United States—Biography. 4. Motion picture actors and actresses—United States—Biography. I. Title.
RC388.5.E973 2013
616.8'10092—dc23
[B]
                                                                    2013018848

13 14 15 16 17   OV/RRD   10 9 8 7 6 5 4 3 2 1

For
Jackson Saint Evans.
Welcome to the family.

To the guy who believed in me . . . when I
no longer believed in myself.

His name, Graydon Carter. Head honcho of *Vanity Fair* and the
epitome of style throughout the world, putting his entire being
into resurrecting filmland's highly controversial bandito.

Reciprocity? Never a factor. There was nothing I could ever
offer him in return.

What allured him to the tale of my bizarre trek? Was it a
shared irreverence for the rules of the game? Doubt it! Whatever
it was, his embrace never ceased to boggle my mind.

It was New Year's Eve, 2004. St. Barth's at its glamorous best.
More than two hundred international luminaries partied away on
Ron Perelman's ocean liner, worthy of a sultan. As midnight approached, my eye caught the silhouette of the man whose presence in my life caused me to be there that evening. There, with
his back to me, leaning on the rail, watching the fireworks as
they lit up the sky, was Graydon . . . alone. I walked over toward
him, and, though I knew he couldn't see me, I heard him utter:

"I know your footsteps by heart, Evans. Remember the night
of The Kid's premiere at the Odeon, in Leicester Square? I told
the audience, 'I've spent so much time researching this man
that, when I die, Robert Evans's life will pass before my eyes.'"

"I remember it well, Graydon," I said. But here was my chance
to ask him what I'd been asking myself for years: "Why me?"

With a wide New Year's Eve grin: "Because I love ya, Kid."

Date: May 6, 1998
Place: 1033 Woodland Drive, Beverly Hills
Time: 8:06 P.M.

Wes Craven has just arrived, Mr. Evans," whispered my major domo through the intercom. "Shall I escort him to the projection room?"

"Try to stall him. I'm running late. Give him the 'A' tour of the house—anything. I'm on the phone with my fucking agent. There are three offers for the book and he's pressing me to take one of them. He's got the wrong author—I don't like any of 'em. I'm holding aces, not deuces. And if he doesn't agree, it's divorce time. Get me on an eight o'clock flight to New York tomorrow morning."

I made my entrance into the projection room, where dinner

was to be served—a full half hour late. Perfect way to start with the wrong foot forward.

There awaiting me was the King of Scream himself, Wes Craven. Bellinis were served. Apologizing for my late arrival, I lifted my glass and made a toast to my guest.

"To you, Wes, one of the few directors in town who is an above-the-title star. Welcome to Woodland."

A bolt of lightning shot through my body. Like a pyramid of wooden matchsticks, I crumbled to the floor.

I was dying.

Lying flat, my head facing the ceiling, I wasn't scared at all. Not in pain. No, I was smiling. In the distance, Ella Fitzgerald echoed: "It's a Wonderful World."

Wes stood over me, ashen. The King of Scream? He was scared shitless. As he bent down to my motionless body, my eyes opened. "Told you, Wes," I slurred in his ear. "It ain't ever dull around here." Then I passed out.

It was only a matter of minutes before I was awakened by a barrage of paramedics. With my blood pressure hitting the lottery, 287 over 140, I knew this wasn't *fly me to the moon* time. Rather, it was looking like *fly me to Heaven.*

In the ambulance, one of the attendants screamed to the driver: "That traffic's gotta move to the side! Put the goddamn sirens on! If we don't get to Cedars ASAP, we got a DOA on our hands."

The multicolored flashing light began blasting away. Moments ago I had heard the fat lady sing. Now, strapped to the ambulance stretcher, I was mesmerized by that flashing light. Through it, I saw the white light zoom toward the sky.

I'm on my way, I thought. *At last I've achieved what I've been looking for all my life: Peace of Mind.*

Hours later, I awakened. Was I in Heaven? No. I was only half right. I did not die. I was reborn. Not Robert Evans, rather Quasimodo, the Hunchback of Notre Dame.

The hours that followed were ER at its best. Hallucinogenic, certainly. I knew that Robert Evans's life, as it had been, was one of the past. White coats by the droves came and went. I was totally immobile, a statue on a marble slab. Not a smile graced a face. It was only a matter of time.

Suddenly, the scan graphs surrounding my cot started oscillating.

A second stroke attacked my brain.

Most think, *Why did this have to happen to me?*

Not me! I was thinking, *Why didn't this happen to me sooner?*

Like a shot out of Hell, my mind flashed back almost a half century, to the day.

I was not in Cedars in Los Angeles, but rather at St. Mary's Hospital in West Palm Beach, Florida, a scrappy, hell-bent kid actor not yet touching his eighteenth birthday. This was no bad dream, but a living nightmare coming back to haunt me.

At that moment, in May 1998, I was lying supine, eyes to the ceiling, in the exact position I'd been fifty years earlier, in May 1948.

It was life-or-death time. My left lung had collapsed. Medically termed a "spontaneous pneumothorax," what I'd experienced was not a disease of the lung, rather a freak occurrence, caused from overstraining the outer pleura of the lung tissue. A bubble bursts, and—like a balloon—so does the lung. Invariably, it's tagged to young Olympians, zealously overtraining in hopes of bringing home the gold.

Mine, too, popped from overtraining. Not for the Olympics, but for every vice I could manage, from gambling to broads. I was on full-blast overtrain! The doctors told my parents that without oxygen professional-style, my lights would have gone out for good. There I was, copping my first part in flicks, and my fuckin' lung pops—from fuckin'! Instead of traveling west, waitin' for my close-up, I'm lying horizontally, waitin' for my lung to fill up.

I never made my high school graduation. Couldn't have cared less. From my junior year on, I'd been given constant demerits for bursting into laughter in the middle of class. They thought I was laughing at them—and I was! Just thinkin' about my double life—a high school junior, kept by three of New York's top show-girls, all beautiful . . . and all double my age. If they'd sent me to a shrink then and there, "delusionary" would have been the call of the day . . . followed by an express train to the nearest psychiatric ward. One full confessional and I would have been first in line for electric shock treatment. Wouldn't blame the shrink—I'd do the same if I were him. Some punk kid, claiming he's known on Broadway as the between-shows fuck of the year?

But it was all true. From the Latin Quarter, to Billy Rose's Diamond Horseshoe, to the Copacabana, the stages of New York City back then were filled with long-stem showgirls. They were looked upon with the same awe that celebrity models are looked upon today. They didn't make the same bread: Two hundred fifty buckaroos a week was the norm. That's for doin' two shows a night, six nights a week, with two hours off between shows. Strange, they all sported mink coats, drove stylish convertibles, and lived in duplex apartments. On two-fifty a week? Well . . . that's where the hitch hitched in.

All of 'em had wealthy "daddies." Those daddies sure in hell weren't married to those "mommies." They were married, though, and that meant they didn't get many nights off to water them long-stemmers. That's where I came in.

What separates a good deal from a great deal is that there

are no losers in a great deal. This was a great deal! Good for the daddy, good for the long-stemmer, and great for the Kid.

Where did we meet? At auditions, where else? My pal Dickie Van Patten and I couldn't sing or dance, but with purpose we trolled the auditions for every Broadway audition castin' them long-stemmers. Between the two of us, we never copped a part in a musical. Never wanted to! But we never missed out on coppin' a phone number. We scored zero with the ones who weren't workin' the Broadway circuit. They were in the market for Daddy Warbucks, not some teenager. But there were enough showgirls out there for our dance cards to stay full.

Poor Dickie couldn't take advantage of his. He was the top juvenile actor on Broadway, going from one show to the next. Never got a musical, but never got a night off, either. Me? I wasn't that lucky. Every Broadway show I auditioned for, I came in second. But I was first when it came to being seven digits away from a good night out. No questions asked. No responsibility. No midnight promises. "Slam! Bam! Thank you, young man!" It was a triple blitz: danger, dropping my pants, and home in time to finish my homework.

It was the naked truth, but I kept it to myself. Learned early in life that continued silence is the best insurance policy for continued breathin'.

And for forty fuckin' years, all that was a secret. Damn it! Why do them down-and-dirties always come back and bite you in the ass? I'll tell you why: When more than two people know somethin', it ain't a secret anymore.

Cut to four decades later, the summer of 1988. It was close to twelve o'clock on a Sunday night. The constant ringing of the phone awakened me from a deep sleep. The guy on the other end was some Italian goombah I knew.

"How the hell are you?" he said.

"I'm out for the night, you dumb guinea. Call me in the morning."

"Well, I ain't. I've been up watching something on television, and I don't believe it. How the hell old are you, anyway?"

I had no idea what he was talking about. I slammed the phone down and fell back to sleep.

The next morning, the lights on the phone were blinkin' as though I'd just won the lottery. But the only payoff was a fuckin' embarrassment! The night before, on *The David Susskind Show*, there was a reunion of long-stemmers. Susskind had invited four showgirls from the old days to reminisce about old times. And then, all of a sudden, right there on national television, they all realized what they had in common: their relationships with the Shaveless Kid.

That was it: In one shot, I had twenty years added to my age.

In the days that followed, I received no fewer than forty calls, each asking the same question: "Don't bullshit, Evans—how old are you?"

My dance card? Forget it! Too old for the field. Thanks, David, for spreading the gospel!

I t wasn't always that way. When I reached the end of my se-
nior year in high school, I knew one thing. The halls of aca-
demia were behind me for good. Hey! I was just eighteen; I
had one lung on hold, and the other ready to pop again. *I might
have a short trip ahead of me,* I rationalized. *I want to taste everything before it's too late.*

That was a long time ago.

It was a sweltering Saturday in the summer of '49. Most civil-
ians were at the many beaches that surround the Big Apple. Me,
I was no civilian. I was an actor on the radio, costarring every
Saturday morning on CBS's top show, *Let's Pretend.*

On the sly, I was seeing a girl whose face graced the cover
of *Life* magazine as the "Debutante of the Year." Naturally, her

parents knew nothing about us. If they had, she'd have been on a one-way trip to a nunnery. Why was she seeing me? Rebellion was the excuse she gave her snot-nosed, pigtailed piglet friends. She knew—and I knew—she was lying. She dug the dirt . . . the dirt of going to Harlem. Being the only white chick in the joint watching shows she shouldn't be watching. Going to the track with me and my pal Dickie Van Patten, rather than finishing finishing school. Sneaking up the three flights of stairs on the Lower East Side to hear Mabel Mercer warble naughty lyrics.

The more she whispered her rebellious acts to her pigtailed piglets, the more they, too, wanted to rebel. She got off on it. Me? I got off on her getting off! If they'd known about it, her parents, icons of New York society, would have gotten off, too . . . with a gun!

In the late forties it was considered chic to spend summer weekends in the Big Apple. Call it inverse snobbism; call it what you want. "With the riffraff at the beaches, we can have the city all to ourselves," long-drawled the snobs. Those were the days, when heritage, not wealth, was the bylaw of society. Wealth alone would buy you entrance only to what was called "café society." But thoroughbred heritage was no automatic pass when it came to big bucks. Many families who dated back to Plymouth Rock were driving Plymouths. "How marvelous New York is in the summer," they'd hoot. The truth was, they'd rather sweat it out than show their hand.

Yeah, but Miss Society's parents had both heritage and wealth. Each summer they'd spend the month of July at their villa in the south of France. It was then I was first allowed entrance into their spacious townhouse on East Seventy-Third Street. Miss

Society was hosting a small Saturday luncheon for a friend of the family . . . and I was invited!

What a joint! The sitting room must have been, I don't know, forty feet high. Outside there were beautifully manicured gardens, right in the middle of the city. There must have been twenty-five or thirty people. I'm thinking, *What's going on? For every guy there's five dames here.* Except for Miss Society, I didn't know any of 'em. It didn't take long to realize their interest in knowing me was nil.

I wasn't taking kindly to the change of air, I'll tell you that. Only an hour earlier, I was signing autographs backstage at *Let's Pretend* . . . Now I'm standin' alone feelin' like a leper!

Finally, an Oyster Bay snob gave me the time of day. With his Long Island drawl on high: "I've been told you're an actor."

"That's right."

"I've never met one before."

Was he putting me on?

"Really," he insisted.

"Well, you have now."

"Are you from England?"

"No . . . not quite."

"Your diction! It's extraordinary! What a luxury to hear the King's English spoken in this city of refugees."

Moving a step closer, I eyed him and half whispered, "You're right, I do speak the King's English . . . King of the Streets, motherfucker." Leaving him with his mouth open, eyes poppin', and face on red alert, I quickly U-turned it to the john for a long-overdue piss. Mr. Oyster Bay? In one big hurry, he scooted from the luncheon.

Big mistake, pal . . .

• • •

A couple of minutes later, the luncheon's guest of honor arrived. What a shocker! He was number one on America's Most Wanted List—to shack up with, that is. His name: Congressman Jack Kennedy, from Massachusetts. He was top honcho on every lady's "heat list." The more he broad-smiled, the wetter them panties got. He knew it, and they *knew* he knew it!

Me, I was by far the youngest guy there. Miss Society quickly introduced us, but the congressman had little interest in talking with an aging teenager. Don't blame him.

Meanwhile, the eyes of every "debu-tramp" were on putter-putter, vying for his attention. The congressman didn't have to ask for any of their phone numbers. They were all given to him before he arrived. Not by his request, rather, but voluntarily by each and every one of those wet panties, all of whom had given up an extended weekend at a summer resort for a shot at being seven digits away from the congressman's call.

Of the twenty-five or so invited guests, seventeen were debu-tramps. The rest, including myself, were invited as shills, so it wouldn't look embarrassing for the debu-tramps or the congressman. Damn it! My first invite to Miss Society's home . . . and I'm a plant!

The clock struck three. Desserts were being served. The good congressman stood and thanked Miss Society for the fun lunch.

Then, wide-smiling at all, he begged an early exit: "It's not easy keeping a seat anywhere these days, much less in Congress. If I weren't running for reelection, I'd take up residence right here on East Seventy-Third Street. But I have to be on the road before the sun goes down, and I promised His Excellency,

Bishop Donahue, I'd spend a bit of time with him before I left for Boston." The congressman had the words down cold. He knew what to say, when to say it, and how to say it.

Wishing everyone good-bye as he was leaving, he took me by total surprise. He actually remembered my name! Impressed? Big!

Yeah, but dumb me, I must have been itchin' for trouble.

"When you see His Excellency, would you give him my regards?"

A dead-ass silence hit the patio. Miss Society closed her eyes, thinkin', *This ain't Harlem. I knew I shouldn't have invited him!*

The congressman, he gave me a triple take.

"You know His Eminence?"

"Very well."

He didn't believe me. His face showed it.

"Very well, huh?"

"That's correct, Congressman. *Very* well."

He was enjoying the confrontation, certain I was lying.

"Join me, then. We'll pay him a visit together."

"Is that an invite?"

"Absolutely!" Then, with a wide smile: "I'm sure he'll take great pleasure in seeing you again!"

We left together . . . by far the best exit of my young life. Them debu-tramps? Their open mouths matched their turned-up noses. What they didn't know was that this actor from the west side of town was not showboating! He did know His Excellency. He knew him well. Well enough to put him right smack in the slammer!

For the record, I was never invited back to East Seventy-Third Street.

• • •

As he drove us across the park to West Ninety-Sixth Street, the congressman threw me a look. "Why did you say that you knew Bishop Donahue?"

"I'm an actor. I like getting reactions."

"I was right! You *don't* know him."

"You are wrong, Congressman! I do know him. I know him well . . . It's a story you don't want to hear."

The congressman's street smarts matched his Harvard diploma. He didn't ask another question.

I had been introduced to His Excellency by my close friend Dino Cerutti, whom I had met through a dime-a-dance girl. I was seventeen then. Dino was twenty-six—a handsome, dashing ex–Army Air Forces pilot who was studying at Harvard Law School. While I probed the streets of Broadway, he probed the "halls of ivy." Strange casting for a friendship, huh? Not really. We both shared one thing big-time . . . pussy on the brain!

The kid from Broadway gave his elder from Harvard one new life. Not one that helps pass the bar exam, but one that opens your eyes to the fact that there is more to life than law—the lawless!

Nicknaming me "Ripley's Believe It or Not Kid," Dino's prestigious family looked upon his new, shaveless friend with, let's say, more than a bit of skepticism. Poor Dino . . . from the moment our friendship began, he became an almost daily visitor to the church's confessional booth. Blame me if you want, but I sure rocked his Ivy League world. Dino tried to rock mine, and rock it he did. He invited me to Bishop Stephen Donahue's domicile.

His Excellency was a close friend to the Cerutti family, who, naturally, were large contributors to the church.

"This ain't no domicile. It's a fuckin' palace on West Ninety-Sixth Street!" I told Dino. I thought I was at the Vatican, visiting the pope! Though he wasn't the pope, His Excellency was considered the second-highest-ranking Catholic in America, under Cardinal Spellman. What followed was, without equivocation, the most bizarre experience of my bizarre young life.

For propriety's sake, I won't delve into the details of what transpired, except to say that what started out as a religious experience ended up a cause célèbre within my family. Stopping my father from having His Excellency arrested and put behind bars posthaste was no easy task.

Back in the young congressman's car, he, quick on the pickup, knew that the kid sitting next to him was one hot ticket.

"You know, Bob, I think it best I visit His Excellency alone. Don't you?"

"If I were you, Congressman, I would."

Pulling out of the Ninety-Sixth Street Transverse on Central Park West, he stopped his car at the corner. I think he felt somewhat guilty. "You know, the visit won't take me more than an hour. How about a hot dog afterwards at McGuinness's?"

"Sounds great to me."

Putting in his clutch, he waved. "See you here at five."

At five fifteen, the congressman and the actor were driving down Broadway on our way to McGuinness's on the corner of Forty-Seventh Street.

I couldn't help it, had to say it: "Congressman, did you give His Excellency my regards?"

"You like trouble, don't you?"

"Yeah! I do."

"So do I."

For the next hour, it was first names all the way.

Over grilled hot dogs splashed with mustard McGuinness-style, and chilled draft beer, the young congressman passed a bit of wisdom my way that all but changed the course of my life. Trying to recall verbatim words and thoughts expressed more than half a century ago would be remiss not only to the reader but to the writer and to the wisdom itself. What I specifically do remember is that I filled three paper napkins writing down, word for word, a brain exercise that the congressman explained to me in minute detail. And then, as we were walking through the revolving doors toward the street, saying our good-byes, he told me something to the effect that "word power is far stronger than muscle power. Stick with it. It could change your life."

It did!

I'd like to say the congressman and the wannabe became good pals.

We didn't. More than a decade passed before our eyes met again. What a decade! He went from congressman to president. Me? I went from screen virgin to the next Valentino. Not quite as meteoric, though. Valentino died at thirty-one . . . and my career did as well. Couldn't help it. I wasn't that good.

It was now the spring of '62. Alan Jay Lerner invited me to a post-theater supper on upper Fifth Avenue honoring the Camelot couple. A Harvard classmate of Kennedy's, he knew my passion for wanting to go eye-to-eye with the then-president once again. Arranging an invitation was no easy task. The soiree was hosted by Flo Smith, an intimate—and I mean *intimate*—friend of the president's. It was supposed to be restricted to ex-Harvard classmates only.

Those Secret Service guys, they knew their service well. They warned the awaiting guests that the president and the first lady would be arriving at exactly 11:40 P.M. Big Ben couldn't have been more accurate!

Earlier that evening, the two of them had enjoyed a rare night out, taking in New York's top comedy revue, a London import, *Beyond the Fringe.* Then, at exactly 11:40, the most glamorous couple in the world made their entrance. Everyone stood. The president and his fair lady shook hands with all. Our eyes met. Our hands shook. Would he remember me? The last time we eyed each other, I had yet to shave. At best, a trivial incident on his historic climb to the top step of the world's ladder.

But that's why he was standing on it: He remembered well! "Did you take my advice?"

"I did, Mr. President."

Smiling Jack got in the final lick. "You must have. I've followed your career closely. Congratulations."

And before I could utter another syllable, the president was off shaking the hand of another he knew far better.

4

Flat on my back in the hospital. Hours passed. I refused to open my eyes. Truth be, I was too fuckin' scared. Hearing the doctors and nurses parade back and forth, whispering their doomsday prognostications. No, I wasn't on my way to Heaven—I was traveling south to Hell.

Keeping my eyes closed allowed me a dreamlike solace. Cowardly, yes, but I was too fuckin' scared to face the reality that awaited me.

A sudden concern was evident. The scan charts surrounding my cot started oscillating rapidly up and down. From the whispered conversations, I gathered I was going through a second stroke—generally considered more lethal than a heavyweight champ at his best.

And that second stroke was followed by a third.

I missed the DOA list, but I was now an odds-on favorite to make DOE: Dead on Exit. As I lay there, my eyes still closed, I could hear the disarray of the specialists, nurses, orderlies, all of whom were waiting for another stroke to blast me. I could almost hear them oiling the zipper on the body bag.

In law and baseball, three strikes and you're out. Life isn't usually that generous, but it was to me. I didn't die. I remained unconscious for more than twenty-four hours, but I was still breathing. Not a doctor in the joint had an inkling of what kind of vegetable I'd end up being.

My first sensation upon awakening was that of a hand touching my arm. "You're gonna pull through, and that's an order." The voice was coming from Sumner Redstone, who had flown out on his private jet to be by my side at this moment of crisis. His voice carried an unexpected charge of reality—not because he was my boss, but because he was coming from a place that only few have ever survived.

In 1979, Sumner Redstone was caught in a hotel room when part of Boston's Copley Plaza hotel went up in flames. He survived by climbing out a window and hanging precariously from a third-story ledge. Only a person with a tremendous will could have clung as long as he did. He was rescued with burns that would have killed a lot of people; they required lengthy and painful skin grafting operations that other men might not have survived.

He bent down, looked straight through my eyes, and whispered: "When I got out of the fire, I couldn't lift a piece of paper. The pain was beyond belief. In those days they didn't have artificial skin. They had to take the skin off the rest of my body. It was horror. . . . And out of that horror? I think I was always driven before, but out of that fire came most of the exciting things I have ever done."

That was no lie. There stood a man who, at seventy-five, lived the energetic existence of an Olympian, a brilliant businessman who was now on the very top of America's corporate ladder, one of the richest men in the world. He had taken Viacom, a small communications company he considered his baby, and built it into the top media conglomerate in the world. His involvement in every company under the Viacom umbrella meant that he followed a horrendous work schedule. It was not unusual for one to wait three weeks to get an hour's audience. And yet here he was.

The memory of his own disfigurement, pain, and immobility convinced Sumner to change his entire work itinerary, and fly out from wherever he was to visit me, sit by my side, in the intensive care unit. He was intransigent: If I willed myself to be functional, he said, to return to normalcy, it would happen. Painful, yes, but if he could do it, so could I.

Each time he left the ICU, the doctors whispered to him, suggesting that he call next time before he bothered to come. After all, it could be a wasted trip. "He's traveling a very thin line," they said. Redstone didn't answer, nor did he call. He just came. Almost every single day. The doctors couldn't make a dent in his determination to see me through. Survival—not white-coat prognostications—was the only thing that mattered to him. Call it instinct, but he knew that at times like these, there's a thin line between life and death. He believed that his passion to overcome mortal adversity could help me find the will to beat the odds.

That belief went beyond friendship or loyalty. It was the quintessential example of character, an all-but-lost quality of human behavior.

How blessed I was to have him in my life at that moment. Without him, I wouldn't be writing this book. Did it tire him? No! It invigorated him. And it saved me.

After Sumner's umpteenth departure from the ICU, I was told by the attending specialists that I'd miraculously pulled through.

In the month that followed, I went through every type of physical pain. The triple-stroke crisis—a miracle? Yes! I was a triple-stroke survivor. But I was also paralyzed on the entire right side of my body, head to toe to tongue. What followed was a month of sheer hell, better known to polite society as "rehabilitation." Days turned into weeks and weeks into months, all of them filled with therapeutic torture administered by the Therapists Three.

I should have seen it coming. For decades, many a practicing doctor had warned me I was pushing the envelope. My ego told me I was immortal. Never feared dying, never feared failing. Illness? Never entered the equation.

Well, that equation made me a statue: a lopsided one. Half my face and body on GO, the other half on STOP. As I said, the right side of my body was paralyzed head to toe, my speech hardly audible. I couldn't swallow food; I was being fed by IVs, decorating my distorted body like locusts on a carcass.

My first thought was to pull them all out—each and every one. After two weeks, I still had the same thought. There was one problem: I couldn't. Not one finger could move one inch.

Strokes are widely, and wildly, misunderstood. There are plenty of half-assed sophisticates who think they know about heart attacks, but those sophisticates rarely have a clue as to the vengeance of a stroke.

A stroke is a brain attack. Mankind's most lethal insult. The brain controls one's entire anatomy, both mentally and physically.

The heart? That's corner drugstore time. It can survive without oxygen for five, six, seven minutes and not only be brought back to life, but fully recover. When heart attack strikes, there's a whole array of techniques—open heart surgery, angioplasty, transplants, arthoscopic operations, and drugs galore—to keep the ole heart a-pumpin'. Heart bypass surgeries are as common today as gallbladder operations.

Ah, but a brain attack—that's different. It still remains, and from all indications will forever remain, earth's greatest mystery. The brain? A millisecond of oxygen deprivation and it's dead. Unlike the heart, once dead, always dead. It leaves no prisoners. Cripples, yes. Ravaging their victims beyond dignity.

Death would be kinder than the rehabilitation many endure.

Supposedly, today we live in the world of atomic medicine, nuclear medicine, PET scans, CT scans, MRIs: This is heroic medicine. State-of-the-art. Doctors can look into the brain and see it at work. They can see a migraine, see the ravages of stroke or Parkinson's.

They know what's happening. But they don't know why. And they don't know what to do about it. Just as we can see a supernova, but we still can't do anything about it.

Comparing the brain to the heart is like comparing Grand

Central Station to a bus depot in Dubuque. The brain runs one, two, and three as the most complicated organ of the anatomy. Just as geologists cannot predict volcanic eruptions, neurologists cannot predict an attack of the brain. What makes it more disheartening is that once the lightning strikes the brain, there isn't a neurologist alive who can do a fuckin' thing about it except talk.

Medical research remains totally clueless to the workings of an organ that accounts for approximately 2 percent of your body weight, and at the same time absorbs 30 percent of its oxygen intake. Yet this tiny organ ravages more human and animal life than all the tornadoes, hurricanes, typhoons, floods, and earthquakes combined.

Despite all talk of progress, I can't help believin' there'll be life on Mars before we figure out how to bring life back to the brain.

One day, a memorable reprieve from such gloomy thoughts: a joyous call from Sumner in Monte Carlo, giving me the details of his glamorous night at the Red Cross Ball, hosted by Prince Rainier.

"I'm sitting here with the royal couple. Next summer I'm gonna enjoy it with you. No buts, Evans! So get to work!"

I closed my eyes. If he only knew the haunting mystery Monte Carlo had played in my life.

My mind traveled back thirty years. It was August 1967. The place: Monte Carlo.

The occasion: the annual International Red Cross Gala, sponsored by her Serene Highness, Princess Grace. The titans of film, politics, industry, and royalty—from around the world they flew for the social event of the summer. More diamonds glittered from below than stars from above. You name 'em, they were there.

A decade earlier, the same gala would have attracted more waiters than guests. What made the difference? The magnetic mystique that Hollywood brings to the party. I know—I was there.

I'd been invited by David Niven and his wife, Hjordis. My evening's companion was no slouch herself. Rather, a princess—not a Jewish one, a real one. Princess Soraya by name. Considered by many the most desired woman in the world, her beauty matched that of Grace at her best. Recently divorced by the Shah of Iran, not because of love lost or infidelity, but rather "fertility, lack thereof." Being royally fucked, yet unable to bear a royal heir, left her enormously wealthy but throneless.

Lucky me! For a fleeting moment—a fleeting month—she was my every fantasy come true.

Sitting at our table were France's most celebrated heartthrobs, Johnny Hallyday and Sylvie Vartan. What a starry table on a starry night in August!

Then, in a flash, the band stopped. A sudden hush. Everyone stood. Their Serene Highnesses made their entrance, sauntering royally toward their table, Princess Grace wearin' that royal tiara to the tens. No one looked, dug, or played the part with greater aplomb. As the band played on, Princess Grace gracefully made her way through the crowded gala toward her most kindred table, all of whom had played a part in her life's journey. First embracing Princess Soraya, she then proceeded to extend a separate welcome to each at the table . . . that is, until it came to me.

Suddenly, memory took a holiday. What a royal fuckin' switch! The princess who was standing there, lookin' straight through me, knew me better than the princess I was with.

Faster than gossip spreads, my mind flashed back eighteen long years, circa 1950.

On my third callback for a juicy role in *Fourteen Hours*, a flick Twentieth Century Fox was shooting in New York, I met a real looker. She too was on her third callback. She got the part—her first. I didn't. But I got her.

Being much sought after, she had little interest in an aging teenager. Yeah, but persistence and good dancing got my foot in the door and her foot on the floor. That winter, we spent many a snowy night dancing up a Latin storm at the Rendezvous Room of the Plaza hotel.

What the looker didn't know was she had a hundred-dollar bounty on her head . . . and I couldn't tell her. How could I? I was the hunter, lookin' to collect the bounty!

For months, my pal Dickie Van Patten and I had been doing everything but ending up in jail trying to meet her. Stalked her digs at the Barbizon Hotel for Women. Tried to bribe Oscar the doorman. No luck on all counts. Finally, Dickie copped a dare. A hundred bucks to whichever one of us got her on his arm first.

So was I dreamin' now? Here she was, dancing in my arms to the beat of the tango. Yeah, but how could I prove it?

Dickie at the time was costarring in Broadway's new smash hit, *Mr. Roberts*. One night, I insisted that Miss Hundred-Dollar Bounty join me in catching Dickie's performance under the guise of introducing her to the director. As the final curtain closed, we quickly hopped backstage. The director? Oh! He must have left early. Yeah, but not Dickie. He was in his dressing room, taking his makeup off. Seeing us walk in, makeup and all, his face paled. There was Miss Hundred-Dollar Bounty . . . on my arm, not his.

The three of us left together through the backstage exit. While Miss Bounty was congratulating Dickie on his performance, I clicked my fingers and a horse and buggy appeared. The Bounty and I climbed in, and off we trotted down West Forty-Fifth Street.

Dickie? Knocked on his ass way past the count of ten.

The Bounty? Some wannabe named Grace Kelly.

My first royal snub. Did it bother me? Not at all. I was with the real thing, not an actress playing the part but a princess whose mystique, beauty, and wealth-by-mistake went toe-to-toe with my old dancin' pal Kelly.

Kept thinkin', *Bad thinkin', Gracie. I was your good luck charm!* From the moment we met, your life traveled north. In those days, you looked at the Barbizon for Women as lush livin'. Scoring a cigarette commercial made you big-time euphoric. Bein' underwhelming in your first flick didn't stop you from express-trainin' it west to heavenly filmic stardom.

What you didn't know, Irish, was that all that success set you up as the perfect mark for one of our century's most masterfully conceived plans. A plan so entrepreneurial and Machiavellian that it went unnoticed in the world's most sophisticated capitals. A road full of treacherous intrigue, promises unkept, romances by order, deceit by command, marriage by design, all led to one road: Catholic Grace Kelly, now Queen Bee of Fickle Flicks.

While you were pluckin' your first feature flick, many worlds away Prince Rainier was heir to the bankrupt house of Grimaldi, the ruling family of an empty monarchy, a minuscule principal-ity less than half the size of New York's Central Park. A comic opera figure living on a tiny rock in the Mediterranean, the des-perate possessor of a throne of anonymity.

With tourism slipping away to the south and scandals within the monarchy running rampant, Rainier's sister Antoinette launched a coup d'état to overthrow her brother, only to have it stifled the morning it was to happen. Rainier's smarts told him it was nothing more than a temporary fix.

Something had to be done. And then, into the void, came a Greek . . . with a vision.

Aristotle Onassis was a penniless Greek immigrant whose ruthless ambition and brilliant vision catapulted him into the international world of finance. By the 1950s, he was one of a small circle of men whose wealth and power gave him a celebrity status in every capital of the world. Onassis's magnetism was overshadowed only by his mystique, a mystique strong enough that it would later mesmerize Jacqueline Kennedy into becoming Jacqueline Onassis. His rise from steerage passage out of Turkey to ownership and control of half the world's shipping had made a giant of this strange, five-foot, five-inch brooding Greek peasant.

What few knew was that Onassis had a partner: The Société des Bains de Mer, a mysterious consortium that had operated the Casino de Monte Carlo for close to a century. Acting under secret concessions granted by Rainier's ancestor Prince Florestan, they controlled the monarchy lock, stock, and barrel for more than a hundred years. By this point, though, the Société was bankrupt, and they fell captive to Onassis's ingenious plan to use their distinguished heritage as an umbrella for a tax-free base.

With his insightful eye for the future, Onassis seized ownership of the Société in 1953. The Casino was his first step in a vision that became an obsession—taking a forgotten jewel, a tiny, impoverished principality, and royally transforming it into a fuckin' money machine.

Well, it didn't quite work out that way. He gambled on them gamblers gamblin' . . . and they weren't showing! Along the Riviera, glitzy new casinos sprang up like McDonald's franchises, while Monaco was shrinking into a prune, suffering its worst year ever. Tourism was off by 70 percent, and without them punters puntin', catastrophe loomed large. The dulled ambiance of Monaco's pebbled beach was beginning to take on the aura of a legend in decline, looked on by many as nothing more than a sunny place for shady people. Onassis's jewel was starting to tarnish.

"What this joint needs is a good crap game," quipped the late, great Edward G. Robinson.

By demand, Onassis gave his Serene Highness his fuckin' flyin' papers. "Get off your royal ass," he told Rainier. "Find yourself a bride."

He was right: The right bride could do the same for Monaco's tourism as the coronation of Queen Elizabeth did for Great Britain. Problem was, pickings were slim. Most every European throne had collapsed by war's end. In looking for a royal hook, the brooding Greek's insight was pure genius, pulling out of the deck the one ace that could bring back the heavy hitters.

What's more royal than film royalty to bring glamour back to the table? Get them punters puntin', them hitters hittin'. Light up them skies with enticing excitement, glamorous galas, wondrous wealth!

Protecting his back, Onassis counseled with Father Francis Tucker, Rainier's personal chaplain and most trusted friend. Though at first he was shocked by Onassis's entrepreneurial gall, the good father was quick to realize that money was Monaco's main industry. Without the prince knowing, Onassis had pocketed Rainier's Rasputin. Allowing pragmatism to overrule patriotism, the good father approached Rainier in a most fatherly way. "My Lord Prince, why not consider a film star who at least would be able to play the role?"

The Greek's next move was to seek the help of his American friend George Schlee to find a box-office star for his unmarried prince. Mindful of Onassis's sober resolve, Schlee called in a long-standing chit on Gardner Cowles, publisher of *Look* magazine. Using his publishing celebrity, Cowles approached the top candidate: Marilyn Monroe.

"Is he rich? Is he handsome? Is he from Africa?" she purred excitedly.

The prince? Who the fuck is he? Monaco? Never heard of it. "Give me two days alone with him," she giggled, "and he'll be on his knees wanting to marry me!"

Told ya diamonds are a girl's best friend! Ah, but timing made her a giggle late. At the same time, in the spring of '55, Grace Kelly and her lover, Jean-Pierre Aumont, were in the south of France enjoying the Cannes Film Festival. At lunch one day, she told him that she intended to skip a photo shoot with the young prince of Monaco. It conflicted with her hair appointment. Appalled, Aumont insisted that she cancel it.

"Grace, he's the reigning prince of Monaco. He's deserving of better manners. You can't be a no-show!"

Poor Jean-Pierre! His princely manners cost him his lady fair!

Our elegant Grace was no stranger to romance. Her white-glove aristocratic exterior elegantly covered a lady. But that didn't stop her costar Gary Cooper from not-so-elegantly labeling her "a cold dish until you got her panties down. Then she couldn't stop exploding." Our Serene Highness was well-known in Hollywood for playing summer camp with most every leading man she flicked with. All but one fell madly in love with her: Ray Milland, Frank Sinatra, Bing Crosby, Clark Gable, and yes, Gary Cooper.

The exception? Cary Grant. He was in love with himself.

Grace was willing. But her wicked ways made her wickedly worry about the medical exam she would need for royal acceptance. Assuring the crown that she could bear an heir was not the problem. Assuring them she was a virgin? That was another story. Giving another Academy Award–worthy performance, she copped to the fact that she was not. But she was Catholic! She was fertile! She was rich! And she was a big fuckin' movie star! Four out of five was good enough to close the royal deal.

To the outside world, of course, assumptions were assumptions. Laughin' inside were many who knew all too well that there wasn't a microscope on earth powerful enough to find a virginal spot on her soon-to-be-royal anatomy. But gentlemen were gentlemen, and the lady's reputation, at least, remained intact.

Onassis oversaw every aspect of the wedding. Couldn't afford to fuck it up. On the day of the nuptial bliss, April 12, 1956, he stood on a shady deck of his yacht with the ship's captain, watching Grace step ashore on Rainier's arm. "A prince and a movie star," he said. "It's pure fantasy."

Speaking of royal snubs, not one of the royal houses in Europe accepted an invitation to the wedding. Equally insulting, not a major nation in the world sent a significant dignitary.

I could have done better on my fourth marriage!

The closest approximation to royal guests at the Monaco wedding were ex-king Farouk of Egypt and the Aga Khan. In true comic opera tradition, Rainier designed his own uniform for the occasion, an assemblage of gold tassels, epaulets, ostrich feathers, and sky-blue trousers. Not so Grace: Hollywood's Best went to MGM to commission a bridal gown with singular style, one that befitted a princely profile.

The royals? "Fuck 'em," laughed Onassis. "The only thing they bring to the party is excess baggage. With or without 'em, my nuptial production will make history." He was right, bigtime! This connubial knot between film and royalty caused the first media superblitz of the electronic age. Onassis wasn't just another pretty face. His one ace, "seduction by demand," flipped the dazzlin' deck, jump-starting a beach pebble into the Hope Diamond, turning Monaco into a Magic Kingdom.

As one decade dissolved into another, Grace's fairy-tale marriage to the prince slowly eroded into a nightmare. What started as Onassis's seduction by demand snowballed into duty by demand, birth by demand, smiles by demand—all preempting her tears of unhappiness. Rainier's ever-worsening moods scuttled their chances for a loving relationship; a lack of communication gave way to indifference and, finally, animosity.

Eerie the irony: A tarnished tiara brings with it many a tearful year. Haunting, the parallels between the two most glamorous royals of our century, Princess Grace and Princess Diana.

Both nonroyal themselves.

Both from privileged backgrounds. Both sparking wide popular appeal.

Both brought warmer, more human touches to their respective royal houses.

One ushered fame and glamour into a penniless principality,

catapulting it into an era of great fortune. The other lent glamour and innocence to an emotionless House of Windsor.

Both provided heirs to the throne. Both were imprisoned by their positions.

Both were victims of failed marriages.

One allowed her crown to prevail . . . the other, her feelings.

Each killed in a car crash, before her time . . . the one prerequisite for pop culture immortality. Being trapped forever in eternal youth suspends one's being. Elvis, Marilyn, James Dean, John F. Kennedy—both the president and his son—demonstrate it best. Each enshrined in the stained-glass windows of pop culture's cathedro-theque.

Royal as them tiaras may be . . .

Heavy are them heads that wear 'em.

Wearing the crown is far more glorious for those who see it . . . than for those who bear it.

6

For weeks, I allowed no visitors in to see me. None. That included my only son, Joshua; my only brother, Charles; my only sister, Alice; and my dear ex-wife Ali MacGraw, a lady I love, and whom I consider one of the closest friends I have had in my life.

Call it ego, narcissism, self-pity, horrendous pain, shame at my distorted face—I knew that seeing them see me, and knowing what they were thinking, would create emotions I was not strong enough to take.

I took some consolation in the steady stream of well-wishes that arrived on a daily basis from the outside world. As soon as the bad news hit the papers and newscasts around the globe, the hospital had been forced to put on an extra operator to handle the overload.

In intensive care, you're not allowed to receive flowers. In the first five days alone, the hospital was deluged with more than a thousand handwritten notes of encouragement. And they kept up, at a rate of hundreds a day, for the entire month that I was there. The one I savor most is possibly the shortest:

> *Dear Bob,*
> *Just heard about your penis implant in hospital.*
> *Congratulations on pulling thru.*
> *Liam*

Liam Neeson knew how to cheer a man when he was down.

After my interminable residence in intensive care, being examined, reexamined, and re-reexamined, the neurological prognosis came down. It was far from cautiously optimistic; rather, it was closer to aggressive pessimism. Every now and then, some muttered comment would reach me: "With his flair for life? Death might have been kinder." At best, they saw, I'd be one impaired cat.

That was their opinion, not mine.

My unimpaired mind knew one thing: I may have had a tennis court, but I'd be watching, not playing. Forget holding a tennis racket. I couldn't hold a knife, a fork, or a spoon. The MRI tests showed slight brain damage, and when it comes to the brain, slight can have huge ramifications. And only time, not doctors, can tell.

The control centers that blanket the brain cause each and

every stroke to be different. No matter what the diploma, it is all guesswork under the prestigious title of nuclear medicine. Why? Because brain damage doesn't heal. Like the Man Who Came to Dinner, once it's invited in, it doesn't leave.

The doctors who treat stroke victims can see, but they can't do. They can't touch the organ they care for, and they can't stop a stroke once it starts. Comforting, huh?

My invasion occurred smack in the middle of my cerebral artery. Almost instantly, it atrophied the entire right side of my anatomy. From my eye, nostril, lips, and tongue, to my shoulder, arm, leg, fingers, and toes, I was in deep freeze. My genitals? Forget about it.

Miraculously, there was good news: My thought processes were fine. In fact, they were on full-time overdrive. Luck be it, my brain missed the bullet.

This was both a blessing and a curse. Thoughts of death outweighed those of life. As the weeks passed, I still refused to see anyone. The ICU assigned their top three specialists, the ones I came to call the Therapists Three: a physical therapist, a speech therapist, and an occupational therapist. They devoted their complete attention to me. Each day I awakened to torture, to hours and hours of rehab, grueling and exhausting. By the end of the day I dreaded one thing: tomorrow.

Finally, a new sensation: my right big toe developed movement. Could it be? The next day, the toe next to it moved. By the end of the week all five of my toes had movement, slight though it was. But at that moment I began to believe that the Guy Upstairs was looking out for me. He gave me the adrenaline to try harder, to not give up. *You're a gambler,* I thought. *Gamble on yourself. Redstone was right, you can make it.*

Within a week, with the help of the Therapists Three, I could take steps. To me, it was the stairway to Heaven.

Walking all the way to the bathroom, I looked in the mirror. I saw someone I never knew. I was a shadow of the living dead. I tailspinned it to bed, put my head under the pillow, and cried like a baby.

My night nurse gently touched my shoulder. "I'm sorry to wake you, Mr. Evans, but there's a lady outside who says she must see you. You'll understand why."

"I can't see anyone," I slurred.

"A Miss D'Angelo. She's dressed as a nurse and says it's very important."

"Beverly D'Angelo?" I slurred.

"I believe so."

My first instinct was to say no. Suddenly I broke into a half smile—a half only because my other side was still on hiatus.

"Have her come in."

I knew why she was there. The year before, I'd caught her at the worst time in her life, and now she was reciprocating. If she'd called ahead of time, I would have shook my head no. She knew it. That's why she was standing at the doorway.

What a difference a year makes.

7

Jack Nicholson and I had flown into Paris from the Venice Film Festival to spend a week with our pal Roman Polanski. Close friends were the three of us, but circumstances being what they were, it had been close to a quarter of a century since Nicholson, Polanski, and Evans had been in the same room together. We spoke by phone often, and we'd all seen each other many times, but always on a one-on-one basis. Every time Jack went to Paris he met with Roman; every time I went to Paris I met with Roman. With Roman ensconced east of the United States on a permanent basis, our complicated schedules never allowed the three of us the luxury of being in the same spot at the same time.

It felt as though it had been twenty-five minutes, not twenty-five years, since we were last together. That's what friendship treasured is all about. It's a rare luxury that few share. We did.

We partied the night away, hitting the sack at four thirty in the morning. Fully clothed and intoxicated beyond the hilt, I passed out on the bed, neglecting to tell the operator to shut off the phone in my room until further notice.

Ring-ring-ring went the phone. I didn't pick it up. It didn't stop. I grabbed my watch, but I couldn't reach it because my head was beating harder than my heart. Hangover Plus. With my eyes closed, I pulled the phone off the hook.

"Who the hell is it?"

"It's Nikki."

It was Nikki Haskell. Shoeless, she barely touched five feet in height. It mattered little. She was always "Big Nick" to me. No one walked taller.

"Nikki? Am I dreamin'? Where are ya?"

"Los Angeles."

"How'd you know I was here?"

"Traced you down."

"Who died?"

"No one."

"Can I call you back?"

"No, I'm leaving for New York in an hour."

"What time is it?"

"It's seven A.M. your time."

"Are you fucking crazy? Call me later."

"I can't, I'll be in the air."

"Call me when you get there."

I was about to hang up when I heard: "Beverly D'Angelo."

Bringing the receiver back to my ear: "What about her?"

"She wants to meet you."

"Yeah, sure."

Nine hours earlier, Nikki told me, she'd walked in the door of Drai's, by far L.A.'s top action nightspot. "Beverly walks over to my table, whispers in my ear. 'Bob Evans—you know him?' 'Of course I do. He's my best friend.' 'I want to meet him. Arrange it.' Kisses me on the cheek and leaves with some gorgeous young hunk who looks younger than your kid. I got her number—take it. I've done my part."

Poor Nikki had to hold the phone to her ear for more than five minutes. That's how long it took to find the light, my glasses, a pen, and a pad.

"I thought you checked out," she said when I got back.

"Don't be a wise-ass. What's the fuckin' number?"

"Well, thank you, Mr. Evans, for doing me such a favor!"

"Sorry, Nikki, I was just in the middle of a great dream."

"I'm sure you were. You're too old for a wet one!"

Hanging the phone up in her ear, I passed out till four.

Now I was up, and thinking: *Did I dream that call?* I turned my head and found a crumpled piece of paper next to me reading "D'Angelo" and a 310 number. No dream. How I'd wished it were.

For years, I'd watched her on the silver screen. Not once did she fail to light it up. Nor did her raspy, naughty lyrics ever fail to light up the Viper Room, where she appeared most every Sunday. Strange, after all those years in the same town, we'd never met. At many a party we'd stood within a hundred feet of each other, yet we never shared a hello. Laughter always surrounded her. The guys doin' the laughin', she doin' the talkin'. Never being one to break up a one-woman show, I walked the other way.

Picking up my call, she had no idea that I was in Paris. Not wanting to give Miss Smart-Ass the edge, I yawned.

"Nikki passed on the message."

"The messenger always gets killed," she puttered back.

"Yeah, she almost did. Poor Nikki, I love her. There's no one like her. Thank God . . . the world ain't ready for another." Yawning again. "Listen, kid, if we're gonna get together . . . let's do it soon before I'm too old to appreciate you."

"Poor baby," she purred back. "I'm working tomorrow and Friday. How about Saturday?"

Before I could tell her I was in Paris, she putter-puttered, "On one condition, lover boy. I know you're a silk pajama man. Let's cut to the chase. No getting-to-know-you stuff. Saturday at noon I'm coming over, wearing my pink silks. Don't be a disappointment to me. Get a good night's sleep on Friday. You'll need it!"

My throbbing head wasn't up to her putter-putter games.

"D'Angelo, if I'm gonna be there to greet you in them pink silks, I've got some big travelin' plans to change!"

"*Shhh.* Change 'em. It'll be worth it!"

Paris? It suddenly looked like Pittsburgh. Good-bye, Jack! Good-bye, Roman! Hello, Los Angeles and pink silks!

On Saturday, at noon, the clock struck twelve, and the doorbell rang. Hello, Beverly in them pink silks! Well, I was half right. The silks arrived, but no Beverly. Instead, my butler, Alan, walked in with a beautifully wrapped package. A three-foot rose was pinned to the top. *What the fuck is this?* I thought. *With my luck, it could be a bomb! Should I open it? Maybe I'll have Alan open it . . .*

He did. Under the tissues were the best-lookin' pink PJs I'd ever seen. But where the fuck was Beverly?

On top of the pinkies was a handwritten note:

Beverly D'Angelo

Dear Mr. Evans,

First of all, I'd like to thank you for accepting this letter—from what appears to be a perfect stranger.

We do, however, have reason for contact.

You see Mr. Evans, I am Beverly D'Angelo's pajamas.

From the moment she told you she'd see you at noon Saturday, I was on her back: "Re-read his autobiography! I urged her. Cancel all plans til the year 2000! I implored. "And for God's sake do something with that hair!"

Now, I must remind you that I am a member—in good standing—of Miss D'Angelo's wardrobe (For many years in fact) It is not in my nature to betray her—my entire life has been devoted to covering up for her.   —cont—

However, her shenanigans This morning, her blatant selfishness, her complete lack of social responsibility have torn the very soul of my fabric.

I must tell you that Miss D'Angelo will not be arriving today.

She has flown to Vomo, a small island west of Fiji.

She left the house at six A.M. Nude. Babbling something about "the tabu isle" native genitilia and Kava juice.

I offer myself no hostage until her return.

Respectfully
Miss D's Pajamas

I read it, and reread it, and re-reread it. Was I pissed? You're fuckin' A! Pissed with myself. Could I have been that stupid?

Fantasizing about Beverly in them pink PJs had flipped me back from Paris to Los Angeles, only to end up with a fuckin' letter, a red rose, and a box of PJs filled with tissue, not Beverly. Taking a long, hard look at myself in the mirror, I realized once more how pussy power has never ceased to fuck up my life. It's been more than half a century, and I ain't learned yet.

Strange, ain't it? In 1958 I'd skipped the set of the Marilyn Monroe picture *Let's Make Love* and flew off to Paris to get engaged to the then love of my life, Danielle Loder. As soon as I got there she dumped me. Forty years later, I fly from Paris to Los Angeles to meet a potential woman-of-my-dreams and end up with a box of pink PJs. What does it prove? You figure 'em out, I can't.

I never told Jack or Roman the reason for my quick exit from Paris. It would have given them too much pleasure.

Nine days later, at ten thirty in the evening, Miss D'Angelo was on the horn. Not wanting to give her the satisfaction of her fuckin' stand-up, I held my temper.

"Great trip, huh?"

"What trip?"

"Fiji."

Bursting into laughter. "I've been in town the whole time! Just wanted to keep you on hold . . . get my house in order."

"You mean 'your guys' . . . ?"

"That's right!" she giggle-giggled.

"Well, thanks. I flew six thousand miles to hold my dick."

"Is it that long? Poor Beverly lost out. Do I get another chance?"

Smart-ass broke my cool. "Them PJs made me opt for takin' a hike. I was in Paris with Roman and Jack . . ."

"You were *where*?"

"In Paris! I called you from Paris!"

I could have gone through the entire Sunday *New York Times* by the time she caught her breath from laughing.

"I . . . I thought you were up the block," she gasped. "You're torturing me. Every time I laugh it hurts! I'm in terrible pain."

"Good. Hope it gets worse."

"Shhh. Lover boy, be nice. I need some TLC bad. I'm in awful shape—lyin' in an orthopedic bed with my leg in a cast. Would you mind letting go of your dick long enough to do a lady a favor?"

"Sure, why not? By this time I can't find it anyway!"

"I'm at the Beverly Prescott Hotel. Sixth floor."

"Who are you shackin' up with?"

"I'd be on my knees to you for a smoke, but my leg's in a cast. It's up so high, it looks like I just kicked a fifty-yard field goal and my knee froze in midair!"

"Put it in the wrong place, huh?"

"Uh-uh, a kneecap floats! Mine doesn't. That's why I'm here! And I'm *dying* for a smoke. Walk a mile for a Marlboro, but I can't walk! They don't believe in cigarettes here."

"What else, madam?"

"Well, if you're going to be Prince Charming, you can pick up a bottle of vitamin Cs. And if you have any Tylenol 3 . . . I'll take that, too."

I looked at my watch. "I'll be there at eleven."

At 11:05 I got out of my car at the Beverly Prescott and told my trusty young right-hand man, Rio, "I'll be back in half an hour. Wait for me."

Armed with cigs, vitamin C, Tylenol 3, and a bunch of roses I grabbed from my sitting room, I went up.

When I arrived, her girlfriend was saying good-bye. I sat on a chair, took one good look at her, and this time it was my turn to burst into laughter—but I couldn't. The lady I had longed to meet for years was lying flat on her back, her leg suspended in the air like an oak tree in free fall.

Before I could utter a word, she looked over at me.

"I look awful, don't I?"

I didn't know what to say.

She put her finger to her lips. "Shhh." Then, curling the same finger, she beckoned me over to her bed.

At seven o'clock the next morning, I snuck out of room 605 and woke up poor Rio, my young assistant. I looked like the walking wounded. Rio rolled down the window.

"Take me to the nearest hospital," I said.

"I can't. I have class in half an hour and I haven't done my homework. You look terrible."

Yeah, but it was sure worth it.

What happened during those eight hours? It's not for me to say, except . . . I never thought so many firsts could happen in one night. Especially with a cripple!

She was also the first lady I ever chose over the city of Paris.

Now, a year later, there she was standing beside my bed. I burst into tears. Couldn't stop crying. Neither could she.

8

With the bedside manner of Hannibal Lecter, Cedar's primo neurologist dropped by on his daily rounds. Pulling up a chair, he nonchalantly gave me news I did not want to hear.

"Robert, I know that patience is not one of your many virtues. Considering the fact that you're totally coherent after three strokes, you've got to consider yourself a lucky man. You took a big hit. Don't expect your life as you've known it to ever be the same."

Acerbically noncommittal, he let me know that there was no way to predict the percentage of recovery I could expect. But his lethal purr made it all too clear that I shouldn't expect any miracles.

"Psychologically, your entire thinking process—your desires, your likes and dislikes—will be permanently altered. Your physical capacity? Well, that's a different story. It's mostly dependent upon how your body and limbs react to your rehabilitation program. I'd be less than candid, Bob, if I didn't tell you that rehabilitation is no day at the beach. Will you have pain? Yes. Will you have frustration? Absolutely. Will you become depressed? Sure, how could you not? It doesn't matter, though. Put it all on the back burner. Rehabilitation is the gold key to a successful recovery.

"I've got a feeling you'll be one of the lucky ones. Can't promise you the extent of your mobility, but with enough rehab—nine months or a year—you could actually walk again. Your mobility might be limited, but we have these new miracle canes now, they've got four prongs on the bottom. Balances your every step. You could actually be able to walk up and downstairs. Not bad, huh?"

The motherfucker wasn't through. He had more good news to shout about. "Monday, you start therapy. You're very fortunate. We've got the top three therapists in the hospital on your case. One for speech, another for occupational therapy, and the third and most important, your physical therapist. She's tough, but she gets the job done. Stick with her. Why? Because we're working against the tick of the clock. It's the first six months, Bob, that are most important. In that time, we can judge, with some accuracy, just how much of your damage is unalterable. I implore you, if you've ever practiced discipline, this is the moment of truth. These six months are vital. After that, your motor nerves and arteries will start to atrophy, becoming more and more inflexible. Once that happens, your body will never be able to recuperate to any discernible degree. We're talking about a nine-month window. That's when the clock runs out. Whatever inability you have then, you will be left with. Forget trying to be cavalier, Bob. Every stroke patient is prone to having another. You can't afford a fourth. It could leave you dead or, worse, a vegetable."

Tapping me on the shoulder with his shitfaced smile, he half-whispered, "We won't get you back as good as new, but we'll get you back." Then he threw his knockout punch. "You mustn't forget you're a different person now than you were before the stroke. You're going to have to accept the fact that you'll be left with no choice but to have different goals, different pleasures." He shrugged his shoulders professorially. "You may even get to like the new person better than the person you left behind."

The more he soft-pedaled my all-but-crippled future, the more he was getting off. Dr. Lecter was one sick fuck. Predicting gloom must have been his kink. Helping his victims envision a life of continued misery, his aphrodisiac.

But my rage at Lecter's diatribe worked—in reverse. Through the clouds of his doomsday forecast I glimpsed a purpose, new hope. My new goal? To get well enough to tell this sadistic white-coater that he wasn't preaching to the converted, that he was talking to the wrong guy. I was determined now to prove his professional expertise dead wrong. I was not going to have the rest of my life determined by what this half-assed brain mechanic thought was "realistic," I hadn't come this far to be sidelined by him or any other miracle medicine man.

It wouldn't be the first time I'd tangled with an eminent doctor.

9

In September 1973 I went toe-to-toe with a doctor whose healing powers were considered mythical by the most sophisticated people in the world.

Throughout that summer, Bobby Riggs had been using my tennis court on a daily basis to practice for his match with Billie Jean King. Being a hustler, he offered every A-plus player in town two games and service for five hundred bucks a set. Tennis players, no matter their level of skill, have bigger egos than serves. All but two were an easy mark for Riggs to pick up a couple thousand a day without breaking a sweat. Yeah, but each and every player got a bit of advice from Riggs in return.

"The dame doesn't stand a chance against me. I could nail my right hand to my back and beat her with my left. That five hundred you just gave up? Forget it. You can make thousands using what I've just told you."

Me? The schmuck, I was his host for the entire summer. After two and a half months of daily hustling on my court, he embraced me. "You've been one great host, Evans. Thanks." Shaking his head, he whispered, "Beg, borrow, steal, do what you gotta do, but give the seven-to-five odds on me. Just spread it out. Don't want them odds to go higher. It'll be the easiest hundred Gs you ever copped."

Well, getting it from the horse's mouth ain't bad. But knowing that he was half horse, half hustler, I decided to put up just half the bread. Gave 7-5 and spread fifty Gs on Riggs.

Riggs? He lost. Me? I still think he was going the other way, picked up his last big payday. Once a hustler, always a hustler.

The event itself had built up such steam that it became the first time in tennis history that a match was played on prime-time television. The Houston Astrodome was filled to capacity, and I was invited to sit in Riggs's box. That made it a fun night to look forward to, especially with my fifty grand riding on my pal Riggs.

Didn't quite get there. Shortly before the match, my brother, Charles, who'd been stricken with a heart attack two years earlier, called me ebulliently. Finally, after a year of waiting, he had been admitted to the Kempner Clinic at Duke University in Durham, North Carolina. Walter Kempner's international reputation was mythical. You needed high political influence, international celebrity, or some other world-class power to gain admittance to his almost holy, four-day clinic. As one decade followed another, Kempner's fame turned to fact. His face graced the covers of every major publication in the world as the purveyor of the single most advanced treatment in modern medicine.

The highlight of Kempner's international reputation was his "rice cure." The Kempner Clinic was situated in the midst of acres of rice houses, where patients lived, sometimes for as long as a year, under the strict dictates of the Messiah. His intensive diet regimen was reputed to offer not only weight loss but also significant improvements in blood pressure and in reduction of heart attack and stroke. His method also improved kidney and liver function and even improved eyesight.

After a year of politicking and calling in every chit that he could, my brother, Charles, was booked to enter the Kempner Clinic on September 18, 1973. Being knighted wouldn't have brought about a more ecstatic reaction.

"Bob, you're coming, too. This is a life-sharing experience."

"Can't, Charlie. I've got fifty thousand on Riggs. I'm going to Houston."

A long silence ensued.

"Bob, I'm scared shitless. I don't want to face it alone. It's my fuckin' ticker. It failed me once. Doesn't bode well at my age. This guy could be my saving grace. Please, be there with me, will you?"

Together we checked in as outpatients, staying at the Howard Johnson Manor directly across the road from the Kempner Clinic.

I never visited a concentration camp, but I'm prone to believe that Kempner did his residency in one of them joints. What transpired during those four days had to be the single most degrading experience of my life. Always sporting a hospital gown, always waiting on line. Was it worth it? Sure, if you're a masochist . . . which I ain't. I don't like needles, but I became a pincushion there real quick. And that was the fun part. Rather than go into detail, I'd rather simply say that every indignity known to mankind was perpetrated on this guy—and I didn't even want to be there. You name it, we got it stuck into us, out of us, and around us.

My brother and I moved from one interrogation to the next, waiting for the SS to grab us and shove another pipe up our asses, down our throats, or wherever else they knew it would hurt. The only thing missing was the tattooed serial numbers on our wrists. Hey, maybe it was worth it. On Friday, we were to meet the Fuhrer himself.

My brother shook his head. "We ain't gonna make Friday." I wasn't laughing. Perceptions can be mighty dangerous. It was only Kempner's reputation that made us stick it out. On the night of the big match at the Astrodome, Charles and I lay on our beds at the Howard Johnson, watching my fifty K go down the drain as Billie Jean King beat Riggs easily in two sets. It hurt, but it came in a distant second to being an inmate at Kamp Kempner.

Our degradation finally concluded, Charles and I got the nod that Dr. Kempner would see us Friday at 11 A.M.

At exactly 11:01, Eva Braun announced, "Charles and Robert Evans." We stood. "Dr. Kempner is ready to see you now."

Behind the double doors, the Fuhrer himself sat behind a large, semicircular oakdesk. No smile. No charm. No pleasantries. Ahh, but with a German growl that would scare the shit out of a Doberman pinscher, he ordered us to sit.

"Vich vun off you is Charles? Vich vun off you is Robert?"

"I'm Charles Evans."

For the next fifteen minutes he sat in total silence, fastidiously examining each and every result of the hundreds of tests my brother had endured. Finally, Kempner smilelessly looked up, turned his head toward one very nervous Jew.

"Charles Evans, you are a ferry sick man."

With that, he stood—I could swear I heard his heels click—and started rattling off a litany of problems. "Charles Evans, you vill not be able to leef the clinic. I am assigning you to Rice House Nineteen. You vill follow my order. You vill not deviate from my instructions. You are a sick man." Kempner began to pace. "A ferry sick man. With your diet and style of liffing, you vill not make fifty. You are lucky to have gotten here in time. With proper care, vee vill bring you back to health. Safe your life. *[Cue mirthless Germanic chuckle.]* Charles Evans, vithout the Kempner Clinic, I doubt whether you vould have made Christmas." By the time Herr Kempner was done with his little monologue, my brother's face had turned ashen.

Herr Kempner then turned to me and rattled off a list of internal problems that were disrupting my entire organic system.

"Robert Evans, you are also ferry lucky. Your internal problems are treatable without being ensconced at the Kempner Clinic. You vill be given the Kempner diet, vich must become your vay of life. If it is not treated vith the proper discipline you vill be in eefen worse shape than your brother. You vill be visiting our clinic on a semimonthly basis for testing. Vee cannot take a chance on any further arterial clotting. You are excused."

"Doctor Kempner, can I have a few minutes with my brother before he takes off?"

"Absolutely, take a full hour if you vish. But you must report punctually at Rice House Nineteen at two P.M."

"No problem, Doc," Charles replied.

The door closed behind us. Grabbing my arm, my brother laughed.

"If that guy thinks I'm gonna be a prisoner in his rice paddy, he's nuts. We're both getting the fuck out of here. Now!"

A plane was leaving for LaGuardia in forty-five minutes. "Come on," he said. "We can be back in New York by one o'clock." We grabbed the first cab we saw and slipped the driver a sawbuck. We hadn't even bothered to go back to our rooms to get our things. "Get us to the airport in twenty minutes. Got it?" We climbed in and he pressed the accelerator to the floor. Charlie couldn't stop laughing. "We're outta here and we ain't never coming back. Fuck our clothes, fuck Howard Johnson, fuck Duke University, and fuck Durham, North Carolina."

Two hours later, we landed at LaGuardia in New York and hailed a cab. A half hour later, our carriage pulled over to the curb on Fifty-Fifth Street and Seventh Avenue. Walking into the Stage Delicatessen at that moment was one of the great highs of our lives. We took a deep breath and breathed the breath of Heaven. It wasn't Heaven. It was pastrami, but at that moment in time it sure felt like Heaven. Grabbing the first waiter we could, we slipped him a twenty and gave him our order: Two double hot pastrami sandwiches splashed with mustard and sauerkraut, surrounded by pickles, a Dr. Brown's cream soda on the side, and a slice of cheesecake waiting in the wings.

To this day, those pastrami sandwiches at the Stage were the best lunch of our lives.

Strange, ain't it? In 1997 it was the eminent Dr. Kempner who died of a heart attack. My brother, Charles, outlived him by a decade. And your author is still putting pen to paper.

10

Four huge hands holding both my arms awakened me from my sleeping hell. In actuality, it was the first step of my new life. Two of the hands belonged to the physical therapist, a guy who made the Rock look like Rob Schneider. The other two belonged to a nurse who could have been in the road company of *Cuckoo's Nest* as Nurse Ratched.

Four hands weren't enough, however, to keep my body from falling to the floor.

In reality, I wanted to fall through the floor and straight to the basement. As the days progressed, I began with the use of braces and therefore hands. I could make twenty feet walking somewhat like King Kong. As they wheeled me back to my cot, that wheelchair never looked so good.

How indelible the moment! I could move my leg, but not stand. I could move my arm, but not hold. Even worse, not a toe or a finger had any movement or feeling. My mouth resembled a roller-coaster track, slurring out a word here, a half a word there, but two words together? Uh-uh.

When you're an inmate of the intensive care unit, you're not allowed any visitors—and properly so. My particular area was very well guarded to ensure both myself and the ICU total privacy. There were two guards at each entrance.

Many hours later, a knock on the door awakened me. It was 10 P.M. I looked up from my cot, and there in the doorway, hair standing straight up, arms outstretched, smiling door to door, was the Irishman himself, Jack Nicholson.

He shook his head, his smile on high from ear to ear. "Hey, you ain't dead, Keed. There's still a lot of pussy out there waitin' for you."

"How did you get in?" I slurred. "They guard this place like the fuckin' mint."

He walked over and lay next to me on the bed. "There ain't nothin' impossible. You know that, Keed. You'll be home before you know it. No more tears, huh? I wanna see ya back chasin'."

Nicholson's uninvited bust-in was a clear violation of the strict rules of the ICU—at eleven o'clock at night, no less—and news of it spread throughout the hospital like brushfire. Within minutes, he was confronted by a nurse and an orderly who politely asked him to leave. Nicholson glanced at the orderly with his Irish smile, gave me a wink, and whispered, "See ya sooner than you think."

It wasn't more than twenty minutes before Smilin' Jack was

back at the door again. Not accepting the impossible, he left the hospital, got into his car, and walked back in like Santa Claus with a dozen king-sized pizzas, one box on top of the other, inviting all the nurses and orderlies in the ICU administrative area to share pizza with him.

Then he snuck back into my room, closed the door, and lay back down on the bed with me for more than an hour.

He had no idea how critical this time was. We laughed, cried, and spoke of the wonderments of life: its pains, pleasures, surprises, and survival.

A little while past midnight, getting up from the bed to leave, he kissed me on the forehead.

"Keed, show 'em. Do it for me. Don't let me down."

He left. I lay on my cot like a living corpse. What was left of my brain felt like exploding. The vision of his half-cocked eyebrow and devilish smile, filled with life and joy, made my heart pound through my chest. "I will not be a victim," I repeated in my head. "I will not be a victim, I will not be a victim."

The nurse came in, took a wet cloth, cleaned my face, and took my blood pressure. "Your pressure's still very high, Mr. Evans." Giving me two pills, she suggested that I watch some television. "It will relax your mind," she cooed. She flipped on the remote, switching from station to station until I nodded my head "yes." It was the American Movie Classics channel. The film *Three Coins in the Fountain* was just ending. She left the room. I stared at the set.

The host of the show was now announcing their next feature.

"Now, American Movie Classics is proud to present the 1957 Academy Award–nominated *Man of a Thousand Faces*, starring

James Cagney, who, as well, was nominated for an Academy Award for playing the late great actor Lon Chaney. Surprisingly, the movie introduces Robert Evans in his first role as an actor, playing Irving Thalberg, famed boy genius of Hollywood. Evans later went on to become a famous producer himself, running Paramount for ten years. Now, *Man of a Thousand Faces*."

A chill went through my body. My paranoia kicked in: *Were they all part of a conspiracy to torture me?*

The screen went dark and the film began. It was the opening scene of the first film I'd ever been in, and here I was, telling the great Jimmy Cagney how to act.

They were all dead now: Jimmy and every other actor in the cast. My fucked-up head told me I must be dead, too. You got it. I was hallucinating. Call it Chinese torture, call it what you want, but my head was in total chaos. I passed out until a nurse's needle jabbed me the next morning.

Am I dreaming? My first instinct was that I was dead, and in Hell. Wrong. I was in Hell, but I was alive.

Half awake, half alive, and totally dazed I uttered my first words. What came out was the nonsyllabic slur of a drunken parrot.

"Mr. Evans, you were that close to being a basket case," Nurse Ratched said, with all the sympathy of an IRS investigator. "But together we're going to fix the basket."

Surprise. A smile crossed her face. She went on.

"First, let's hope we can get that tongue wagging again. That's my job."

Closing my eyes, I thought: *I'm dreaming it. I'm dreaming it. This can't be happening to me.* This was my introduction to being a freak of nature. Call me Quasimodo. Can't I close my eyes and not awaken? Go back to playing with Jimmy Cagney, wherever he may be?

This was the first step in what is kindly called the world of rehabilitation. Three hours daily learning to regain the mobility of my two right limbs, five fingers, five toes, my right eye, the right side of my mouth and tongue, and continually testing the function of the left side of my brain.

Then it was on to speech therapy. It ain't easy doing Shakespeare when the right side of your mouth droops like a ski slope, and the left side of your tongue has a perpetual hard-on.

"It's a slow process, Mr. Evans. But it's my guess that, if we work hard together, within six months your speech will be sufficiently audible to lead a normal life."

Easy for her to say. Normal ain't what I was used to. Breaking barriers was.

Guantánamo Bay was a walk in the park compared to the torture I was put through for the next ten days. Was it working? Enough for me to allow my son, Joshua, to visit me for the first time.

Two days later, I invited him back to watch the last episode of *Seinfeld* with me. I thought we could watch it together without it being morbid, that we could have a laugh or two watching Jerry's highly anticipated final bow. Before he arrived, I made sure my hospital room was lit like a set. The lights were dim, the television set was on. I wanted to save him the embarrassment of looking at my asymmetrical face. He arrived five minutes before airtime, kissed me. We both had tears in our eyes but didn't say anything. He sat on the bed as *Seinfeld* went on the air. I put my hands on his, but didn't look at him directly. Didn't want to.

Was the show funny? I don't remember. Frankly, I was too nervous, too concerned about my kid. Did I laugh? Yeah, if you count a half smile. It was better than slurring.

Then, abruptly, the screen went black for an emergency announcement. Frank Sinatra had just died.

At the same hospital where I was still living.

Onscreen they showed the cameras poised outside the hospital, waiting for the gurney to be wheeled out. I immediately buzzed for the nurse and asked her which suite he had been in. She said, "I'm not supposed to tell you, but I will. He died in suite eight-oh-five."

My suite was 815.

I immediately flipped through the various news stations. We missed the end of *Seinfeld*, but my son understood. Each station had a camera at the exit of Cedars, where the Chairman himself was being wheeled out. I was totally silent. My son knew of my long, bumpy relationship with Frank, and here we were a hundred feet away from each other. Him being wheeled out, me being strapped in.

Frank played a very important part in my traveling north in the business. It was among the most bizarre relationships I had in my entire career. What an extraordinary guy! Like no other I've ever met. Being on his good side was Heaven; on his bad, Hell.

Me? I went from Heaven to Hell and back during those years.

11

Kid, you remind me of me. Been watching you close. They tell me you're comin' off great. Been around long enough to have a nose who's going to make it and who ain't. You got a shot at going all the way. Take some advice from a guy who's never learned. When it comes to those hangers-on, though, take my advice: Have your radar on high."

The words were coming straight from the mouth of the King—Frank Sinatra, by name—having a mano a mano powwow at Chasen's, his favorite restaurant in town.

It was spring of '59. He was a megastar playing the lead role in the filmization of the Broadway musical *Can-Can*. Me? A punk starlet, playing my first starring role in *The Hell-Bent Kid*, a western remake of *Kiss of Death*. Screen-tested and plucked it away from many. *Can-Can* and *The Kid*—hell-bent, that is—were shooting on adjoining soundstages at Twentieth Century Fox.

The laugh being that it was *he* who sought *me* out, and with purpose, not by mistake.

Curiosity killed the cat? Well, curiosity all but killed the King. Not that he was losing any sleep wonderin' whether Evans the actor would be the next Laurence Olivier. He was wondering, though—and not smilin'—how does a punk kid not yet hitting the quarter-century mark end up in the biblical sense with the two great loves of his life? Adding insult to injury, the Chairman's spies told him I'd been seeing both of them at the same time. Their names? Ava Gardner and Lana Turner.

Was I impressed that Frank Sinatra was seeking my company? Big-time! Over Chasen's chili and a cold draft beer, it was evident why the crooner would later become known as the Chairman. In his effort to extract information, he opened up his vaulted thoughts, caressing the new kid in town with glimpses into Frank's World.

"Those hangers-on I told you about? Don't be fooled by 'em. There's not one who's not going to hit you when you start makin' it. Your ego tells you them dames are dying to fuck you. They are, yeah—but you're the one who ends up gettin' fucked. Hit up for every penny you've got. Need wheels, rent—you name it, they'll ask you for it. If it ain't a dame, it's a guy, a relative, an old pal. They come out of the woodwork, need a temporary fix: fifty, a hundred, five hundred, a thou . . . Pay you back in a day, a week, a month? Don't matter. Don't loan 'em. *Give.* Give 'em half. That's only if you wanna. If you don't, then be tough about it, not like me. Tell 'em one, tell 'em all, you don't believe in loanin'. With loanin' comes losin'—losin' a friend, that is. If they don't like the answer, fuck 'em. They ain't worth knowin'."

Gulping down a straight shot of scotch with his beer, he shook his head. "Never fails. Every time I lend a buck, I lose a pal. No one's fault. That's not true. It's the fault of the guy who loans. He knows better. You ask when you're on empty. Most of them have intentions to pay ya back. They don't want to lose your friendship. But few of them actually come up with the money. Where are they gonna get it? Close friend, close relative—don't matter. When you can't pay back the marker, embarrassment causes estrangement.

"You know what happens from estrangement? Disdain. Not from the guy who loans—from the guy who owes. Take it from a guy who's loaned big. Lost big, too. Whenever I don't stick to my preaching, I'm the loser. A year don't go by without me erasin' names from my invite list. Never fails. It's the loaners ten-to-one over the field that the eraser hits.

"Giving half, that's different. It don't stay on the record, stops 'em cold from comin' back for more, and everyone's conscience is clean. And don't forget, it's the first half that's always the toughest to get. Once they get it and don't owe it back, the second half's easy to borrow. They can put the first half up as collateral.

"Don't be like me, Kid, spreadin' your legs for everyone. Even when you give, it ain't appreciated, it's envied. If you wanna play Santa Claus, it's your call. Give 'em half if you want. But *don't loan*. Got it?"

Got it I did. The Crooner's wisdom was welcome, and I sucked it up like quicksand. Didn't fall prey to it, though. What he didn't know was, before graduating from his teens, street smarts taught me, the Comer, that continued silence carries with it continued breathing. Whatever Frank's innuendo regarding Ava Gardner or Lana Turner, it was handled with polite evasiveness. So seductive the power of pussy, that unbeknownst to us both, it started a friendship that was both life- and career-changing, not only to the Comer, but to the Crooner as well.

Years passed. It was 1965. *Von Ryan's Express*, starring Frank Sinatra, exploded onto the cinematic scene, express-trainin' it to Blockbusterville, making it Twentieth Century Fox's number-one film of the year and sending Sinatra's cinema appeal to stratospheric heights. Whatever Frank wanted, Frank got.

At that same moment in time, with my cinema career at a standstill, I opted for a shot on the other side of the screen. I wanted to be the next Zanuck, not the next Troy Donahue. I knew one thing: I had to own something to get my foot in the door.

Five thousand buckaroos got me an option on a first-time author's novel, *The Detective*. Call it luck, call it a freak mistake, call it what you want. The novel took off. Became a number-one bestseller. Everyone wanted the rights to the property. No one wanted me. And whose foot got me in the door? Frank's. Imagine being offered north of half a million to take a walk. Not bad. A hundred times my investment! Not good, either. I wanted in, and *The Detective* was my calling card. An expensive one, too: In them days, a half a million was heavy. John Wayne, cinema's top macho star, wasn't pulling a half a million to star in a flick. It wasn't generosity that bountied them half-a-million-dollar offers, but rather a fervent desire to get rid of me.

Was it tempting? You bet your ass it was. But I'm a gambler. With Frank's foot in the door, I had a shot at blockbuster time. The gamble may've been heavy, but making it into that exclusive club on your first shot ain't a bad payoff if you win. And you don't win by playing it safe.

Prevailing friendship dictated that I should send my new-found bestseller to Chairman Sinatra, giving him and his capos first look. You see this in movies, but in real life?

Within seventy-two hours, there I stood, a virgin, with the King on his knees proposing. Desperately digging *The Detective*, Sinatra made it loud and clear to all that the title character, Detective Joe Leland, was his and his alone to play. Immediately, he express-trained it to director Mark Robson, who maestro'd *Von Ryan's*. Before sun turned to darkness, Robson committed, shaking hands with Sinatra that *The Detective* would be their next filmic endeavor together at Twentieth Century Fox, their home studio.

There was one problem: Me. I owned it.

The top studio honchos at Twentieth did not take kindly to the news that Pretty Boy Evans was the novel's proud proprietor. Unsure whether to laugh or shudder, they upped the offer to rid themselves of me. "Am I this diseased?" I thought to myself. "Let's find out." Hey, as a half-assed actor, Twentieth was my home for six years. Guess I didn't leave much of an impression. Not realizing the more they offered to buy me out, the more insulted I was. Without Sinatra attached, I knew full well I'd be barred entrance to the studio commissary. But the Chairman was committed, and I came with the package.

Tired of being pissed on, I let spite prevail. Clenched jaws and all, the suits let their fear of losing Sinatra overcome their pique over my outlandish demands. Starting with a suite of offices in their elite building. For a virgin producer? Is he crazy? Yes, but I got it. The announcement of a three-picture deal with the studio. The first being *The Detective*. Grudgingly, they called their head of publicity to write up the announcement for my approval. The last of my demands was met with a rebellious "No!" A call from Sinatra's consigliere, Mickey Rudin, turned that into a tight-lipped "Yes."

Every actor's fantasy: The studio took out full-page ads in *Variety* and the *Hollywood Reporter*, with photos of the top honchos, from Darryl Zanuck on down, surrounding me as I signed an unprecedented production contract. The headline read "20th Century–Fox welcomes Robert Evans back to the studio as producer of *The Detective*."

To this day, both *Variety* and the *Reporter* hang above my desk. Till this day it remains the money shot of my career. You don't get many. When you get 'em, savor 'em, enjoy 'em. Whenever I'm feeling low, which ain't too infrequent, I look up at them forty-year-old ads. Wham, bam, there I am—smilin' wide again. Never fails.

The Crooner, his porcelain beauty bride, Mia Farrow, and I champagned to the tens *The Detective*'s closure at Fox. Rarely had a case been solved that quickly. And never did a case come back to bite me so viciously on the ass. Pussy power was what brought Sinatra and the wannabe together. Pussy power was what tore Sinatra and the newly appointed studio chairman viciously apart.

With whirlwind speed, before spring turned to summer, I

called a press conference at the Bistro restaurant. There I announced the making of the life story of Maurice Chevalier, scripted by the Academy Award—winning writer Maurice Richlin, starring Alain Delon and Brigitte Bardot. Having both Chevalier and Delon, who was my houseguest at the time, in attendance answering the bombardment of questions thrown at them by a frenzied press corps gave credence to my ambitious undertaking. There wasn't a newspaper in the world that didn't headline the announcement in their entertainment section. Soon after that, I acquired the film rights to *Sam Sheppard on the Run*, a true crime story that soon became the hot new nonfiction book of the year. Paul Newman and Steve McQueen both vied for the role of Sheppard, whose story was the basis of *The Fugitive*.

Lady Luck must have been touchin' me that year. *The Achilles Force*, an original screenplay I'd commissioned Leonard Hughes to write, caught the eye of John Huston, who fell hook, line, and camera in lust to put it on the screen. With Huston in the maestro's seat to direct, it forced the honchos at Fox to announce yet another flick for their virgin producer.

Something's wrong here, thought the bigwigs at Fox. *In three months, the kid's caused more of a stir behind the scenes than he did in a decade on the screen.* In those days, actors weren't given much respect, especially those whose profile and smile prevailed over their talent.

Then, over dinner one evening, the Academy Award—winning screenwriter Abby Mann, who at the time was scripting the filmic version of *The Detective*, introduced me to Peter Bart, the Sunday *New York Times*' ace cinema journalist.

With typical journalistic cynicism, Bart was suspicious. Was this new kid on the block just generating a lot of puff, or would there be proof behind the zeal? He got the proof. Before spring turned to summer, there I was, chronicled by the *New York Times*: "Hollywood's New Wunderkind."

All before I'd made a single picture.

Me, I'm scratchin' my head, thinkin', *How can you be a wunderkind and still a virgin?* It didn't matter. The printed word spreads faster than fire. From virgin producer, I'm catapulted into King of Paramount. All because of a five-thousand-dollar option on a first-time author's work, coupled with Chairman Sinatra's love song to Joe Leland, detective.

Truth's truth: I was far better prepared as an actor becoming a so-called movie star than I was a virgin producer becoming King of the Studio. Had 'em laughing in the aisles. Vegas had me a three-to-one favorite not to make year's end. Forget the fact that I beat the odds. Without Chairman Sinatra's embrace, I seriously doubt I would have ever made it to the field to be bet against.

Then my incident-prone nature came into play again, throwing me the kind of curve few could survive. By this time, I had *Rosemary's Baby*, my pet film project at Paramount, and *The Detective* slated to start principal photography—at approximately the same time. Seem inconsequential? Not so! It had consequences big-time, starting a blaze that spread with a vengeance, leaving behind it havoc, both life-threatening and life-changing. Why? The power of the pussy: in this case, the ethereal Mia Farrow.

Both Mark Robson and Frank Sinatra were on high, anxiously expecting Mia to be Frank's leading lady onscreen, as she was in life. But Roman Polanski envisioned the theatricality of Mia's fragile beauty giving birth to the Devil's own.

What happened? Sinatra's ego went into shock when his lady fair opted to play mother to the Devil rather than putter-putter to his Detective. Didn't sit well with Chairman Sinatra. And *that* didn't sit well with the new chairman Evans. From years of embrace, instant acrimony exploded between The Chairman and the Chairman.

I wanted out. An actress is an actress is an actress is an actress. But I was too late. Professional smarts prevailed over family loyalty. Ethereal Mia tasted immediate stardom, leaving Sinatra hot beyond heat. Should have remembered his own advice: *Don't try to figure 'em out. You can't.* His acrimony turned to umbrage. Not toward Mia, toward me. Hey, Frank, we both know Lady Mia was no innocent bystander. It didn't matter; I was the guilty one. There was nothing I could do except close the picture down . . .

. . . which I couldn't.

Ugly the irony: The film that gave me my entrance to that elusive inner circle, and catapulted me into instant power, was now causing instant pressure to the marital bliss of the guy responsible for my jumping up the ladder.

Rampant ran them emotions. By now, the tension between Sinatra and his lady fair had erupted into open warfare. By dictate of the Chairman: "No negotiations. Total capitulation or you can drop the name 'Sinatra.'"

By now we were six weeks into principal photography. Rosemary was giving birth on the screen and causing havoc in the streets. The Chairman's verbal threats turned into formal legal notice. For her real-life marriage to prevail, her cinematic pregnancy would have to abort. Gotta believe babies always win out.

Rosemary's did, bringing about a visit to the Paramount sound-stages by the Chairman's consigliere Mickey Rudin. Interrupting a highly emotional filmic moment, Rudin served the expectant mother with her true-life walking papers. This was no on-your-knees *forgive me* time, no tears, no copping pleas, no recriminations, and no second time around . . . it's over and out.

Adios, Mia. Evans, watch out.

Chairman Sinatra let it be known loud and clear, in any and every circle that mattered, that I was the rat fink responsible for wrecking their marriage. Restaurant, party, you name it—whenever Sinatra's presence was expected, I got the high sign to stay away.

Not only did the heat not subside, it went from back to front burner. For good reason: *The Detective* and *Rosemary's Baby* opened on Broadway on the same fuckin' day in June 1968. And everywhere it counted—from film critique to box office—*Baby* sizzled, *The Detective* fizzled.

After the handwriting was on the wall, Porcelain Mia shocked me by requesting a "fragile" favor. Call it cat claws, call it a fuck-you to a loved one lost, her ethereal petition was to have Paramount take out a double-page ad in the *New York Times*, *Los Angeles Times*, *Variety*, and *Hollywood Reporter* comparing the dual openings of their pictures, in terms of box-office dollars and critical acclaim. I gave her request the heaviest thumbs-down I've ever given. Thanks but no thanks, Mia. I'm not looking to wake up with a vacancy between my legs.

Not long thereafter, it was Gunfight at the O.K. Corral time. The place: Ruby's Dunes restaurant in Palm Springs. We collided. The restaurant cleared. There we stood. No guns, but plenty of language. When it came to letting off steam, it wasn't easy going toe-to-toe with the Chairman. I did. The more we vented, the dumber we looked. Two sophisticated guys acting like junior high school losers. Sinatra's tirade was such that he ruptured a vocal cord, putting him out of action for more than a month.

It was the late sixties. Flower child time. And mystical Mia towered tall as the quintessential flower girl. When she made another, more flowerlike request—that I lend her the sanctuary of my hidden garden under my multi-hundred-year-old sycamore tree for her birthday party—how could I refuse her? She was Rosemary, the "mother" of Paramount's biggest flick.

I wasn't invited myself, so that night I joined Sidney and Bernice Korshak for dinner at the Bistro. Upon returning home, Sidney and I ventured past the pool toward the projection room. Looking yonder, fifty or more flower children were partying on the grass. And it sure smelled like grass. That pungent aroma hit us both. Sidney grabbed my arm. "You're getting out of here." Without even saying hello to the birthday girl, I Carl Lewised it to the Beverly Hills Hotel for a safe night of sleep.

With every blue sky, there's always dark clouds. The more awards Mia plucked for playing mother to the Devil, the more devilish Sinatra's acrimony toward me grew. We spent the next four years in red flag time. Only once did the white flag rise, and that was for an afternoon only, allowing us both to attend our mutual friend Charlie Feldman's wedding. By the time the sun set, the red flag was wavin' again.

Finally, though, we discovered that time does heal all. By now, it was 1974. As I was sitting down to dinner at La Grenouille, Sinatra walked over to my table as if nothing had ever transpired between us. With royal aplomb, he congratulated me on making *Chinatown*. Asked me to join his table. I did.

An hour later, we left together. Walking to his awaiting limousine, Frank shook his head, laughin'.

"Remember that night at Chasen's?"

"How could I forget?"

"Gave you some good tips, huh?"

"Saved me more green than my accountant ever did."

As the chauffeur opened the back door of the limousine, Ol' Blue Eyes threw me a half smile. "Dames! Sayin' nothin', they're more seductive than any lyric."

Stepping into the backseat of his limo, he lowered his window.

"Strange, ain't it?" I said. "Pussy power. There ain't nothin' stronger."

Our eyes met, and Ol' Blue Eyes shook his head. "Can't fight 'em, they just don't play fair." He started to roll his window back up. "Stay in touch, huh?"

I will not stand at your grave and cry.
For you are not there.
Your soul will never die.
I love you, dear Sidney!

Thus ended the longest, most heartfelt eulogy I have ever given. Date, January 22, 1996. Place, Hillside Chapel, Los Angeles. The deceased? Sidney Korshak.

Those words were triggered from the emotion of sharing forty years of each other's most sacred secrets. Do I remember them secrets? Of course not! Never did, never will . . . except for them that add credence to his myth. The one sentence that best describes "the Myth," as Sidney was called by many who know him, or said they did:

He was, and remains, the single most seductive person ever to cross my life's path.

Was he charming? Not particularly. Was he funny? Not particularly. Was he verbal? Not particularly. Was he a magnet? His presence in any room, no matter city or country, stopped it fuckin' cold! Cold good or cold bad? Depends who was in the room.

Unlike the classic charmer, Sidney's persona was not cultivated, not calculated or educated, neither taught nor bought. Growing up in the streets of Chicago, he was nicknamed by family and friends the *Shtumer*, Yiddish slang for "the silent one." "They bull's-eyed me good," he told me more than once. Until the moment his eyes closed for the last time, he was always the same.

On December 29, 1996, the last Sunday of the year, the *New York Times Magazine* devoted its year-end issue to its annual feature "The Lives They Lived: Some People Who Made a Difference and Why." Between its covers, author Eugene Kennedy chronicled the life and death of Sidney Korshak: his power, his style, his myth. In particular, his dealings with Estes Kefauver, the ambitious senator who was planning to bring his televised organized crime hearings to Chicago. Kefauver's ulterior motive? His presidential candidacy.

"After a few secret meetings," the *Times* piece noted, "Senator Kefauver suddenly departed, without ever gaveling his public hearings to order. An associate later claimed that Korshak showed Senator Kefauver a compromising picture of himself with a young woman. A sting orchestrated by the young Chicagoan . . ." That was the end of the hearings.

Kennedy continued: "As Heifetz was to the Stradivarius, so Sidney Korshak was to the telephone, on which he did more business than most lawyers do in a lifetime in their offices."

Jackie Presser, the late Teamsters president, looked up to Korshak in awe. "There's nothing he can't fix. He don't even have an office. He don't even have a briefcase. He keeps everything in his head. No wonder Sidney's mystique still gives old acquaintance amnesia. When called to repeat anecdotes they once told freely, they respond, 'I don't seem to remember that,' or 'I heard Sidney died. I didn't hear he was buried.'"

Billy Friedkin, the Oscar-winning director—one I yearn to work with again—has plagued me for years with pleas to collaborate with him on the story of the Shtumer. The *Real* Godfather. The definitive story of power in our time.

"I can't make it without ya, Evans. You're the only one alive who has the keys to open them locks. Tell it as it really is."

Billy's not wrong. He knows only too well, though, I'd stop a bullet to protect them down-and-dirties from ever hitting the silver screen.

The Myth and the Wannabe met in the early fifties. *It was love at first sight.* For the next quarter of a century, we were quintessential godfather and son. There was not one month of one year when we didn't share at least an hour a day together. When geography prevailed, "the horn" was our connective tissue.

How proud the Big Man was of his godson. Always at my side, helping my ascent from aspiring actor to studio head. Wherever we traveled, it was seat-to-seat. Whatever the hotel, it was suite-to-suite. Every secret we shared, it was whisper-to-whisper. From the highest echelon of corporate hierarchy to the side streets Mulberry to society's royalty, I was Sidney's kid.

"Hurt Bobby, hurt me!" he said more than once—to people who weren't used to such warnings.

In turn, he lived somewhat vicariously through my adventures—ones he could never afford to indulge himself. Our relationship became the stuff of folklore—not just of Hollywood folklore, but of intrigue at the international level.

Was he famous? Or infamous? Depends on who you asked. Never once, in all the years I knew him, did he grant an interview to anyone. Nor did he let anyone take his picture—except behind my Woodland gates!

Though he was much-gossiped-about himself, the Myth was always short on gossip about others. From the early fifties—the time of Marilyn Monroe, Ava Gardner, Lana Turner, and Kim Novak—into the early eighties, most every above-the-title glamour queen shared the same fascinated desire to meet up with the Myth. And, more blatantly, to know the Myth, and know him well.

It never failed to shock me. Married, unmarried, it mattered little. What really happened between them? I never knew. I never asked. Would you?

Up there on the podium, that day in January 1996, I reflected on an embarrassment I'd carried with me for sixteen years concerning the Myth and myself:

"For more than a decade now, Sidney and I have shared

friendship"—that's right, just friendship—"where love once blossomed."

Holding back my tears: "He dumped me . . . He was right! I was caught cheatin'. When I got in trouble, I made what remains, till this day, the single worst mistake of my entire life: not to call my godfather when I needed him most."

Later, at the burial, a world-famous entertainer embraced me, asking if we could have a chat back at my home. Of course, I said. But once we got there, it was no embrace.

"I'm glad you were honest, Kid. Paid your respects. Made peace with the Big Man."

Then, right smack in the cojones, he whispered hoarsely: "You may not know it, but *you broke his heart*. Your bullshit excuse for what you did? He never believed it. I never did, either. No one did. You're too smart to be that dumb."

"You're right. But I was."

"Bullshit!" Thrusting his forefinger into my shoulder, he forced me into a chair, then started ranting at me. "I was picked up on the same fuckin' charge. Cuffed, right smack in the middle of my performance. I'm allowed one phone call. I call the Big Man . . . and I'm out in half an hour. And I was *fuckin' guilty*."

With an angry laugh: "You, his pride and joy, and I know you were fuckin' innocent. And you don't call? It don't add up. Never did. You were three thousand miles away when it went down, and you cop a guilty plea? A retard ain't that dumb. Like locusts, all of the Big Man's friends came out of the woodwork. 'How could you let this happen to Bobby?' they kept sayin'. You know Sid's ego. He don't look well on being looked down on. This went on for *years*. They had one fuckin' field day with him."

My guest just shook his head. "Every time your name came up, Sid got hot. Didn't want to hear it."

Finally, I jumped up in rage. "Cut it, will ya? I don't need to hear this shit. I said it at the chapel: *It was the worst single mistake I made in my life!* Now, I don't care who you are—get out of my house!"

He shrugged. "Don't feel comfortable being here, anyway. Never liked ya, and I really never liked what you did to Sid. When I heard about the tough times you were havin', I got my nuts off."

Then, instead of leaving, he seemed to think twice, and took two steps toward me. Instinct told me I was about to get whacked. Instead, he put both his hands on my shoulders. "I look at you different now, Kid. Standin' up this morning, speakin' the way you did. Not cheatin' with the truth. Gotta hurt like hell."

"It didn't. It felt good!"

Our eyes locked. "Know how you feel. I miss him, too. My hat's off to ya, Kid." Then, shocking: a kiss on the cheek. "He heard ya, Kid. Just wanted you to know."

He left. I sat. Minutes turned to hours. Silently, I faced a blank wall. Thinkin', thinkin', thinkin', until darkness prevailed over a once-sunlit room. In sixteen years, I hadn't made it from one full moon to the next without jumpin' up from bed in a cold sweat, my heart drummin' through my chest, from the same continuing real-life nightmare: having my family dictate my future, denying me my constitutional right of counsel, not allowing me to call my godfather when I needed him most.

Worse, I let 'em!

Forgive me, Sidney, for cheatin'!

13

"top! Stop! I can't take it!" I slurred out with all my strength. "Stop!"

It was my third week of rehab, and not a day passed when I wasn't discovering a new form of pain. Them doctors and so-called specialists walked through my doors each day, more than a brothel could handle.

The karma that surrounded my ICU boudoir made a graveyard seem like Disneyland. Without exception, the specialists prognosticated a future that scared the shit out of me, but it only made my resolve stronger. The more they kept telling me about my somber future, the stronger my will and the more I kept telling myself, *Fuck 'em. The Kid's gettin' outta here, and it ain't gonna be in a black bag. I'm blowing this joint for good! Got it, motherfucker?*

At least I was half right. I did get the fuck out of Cedars, and sooner than anyone thought. I couldn't walk it, but I wheeled it out. And it wasn't in a black bag.

Behind me was an entourage of three headed by Tamara Sosnick, a professor of physical therapy at Mount St. Mary's College in Los Angeles, and who is considered to be among the top rehabilitation honchos in the country. Her specialty was using an integrated approach of physical, cognitive, psychological, and functional rehabilitation. Bottom-lining those fancy words, she was a masochist's ultimate fantasy. With her were her two sidekicks: Maria, whose specialty was occupational therapy, and Sarah, a speech therapist. When half of your tongue is paralyzed, you sure in hell pray for the best!

The thrill of arriving home was short-lived. Now that I was out of the hospital, I realized, the Three Musketeers would have me all to themselves. I was on full-time therapy. Pain therapy, that is. My limbs, fingers, toes, tongue, and lips were all twisted and stretched as if I were a piece of clay. Every part of my body was being personally manipulated by one of the Three Angels of Pain.

One morning, Tamara was stretching my atrophied right leg. The pain was such that it touched off a hysteria. Try as I might, I couldn't stop crying. Tamara stood by watching impassively. Then, suddenly, she grabbed me by my shoulders—not to comfort me, but to shake me into the truth.

"Now *cut it!*" She held me firmly until my hysteria settled and my crying stopped.

Then, without a smile, she gave it to me straight. "If you've got a chance at all to recover to normalcy, we're working against a mean clock. It's a very small window, six to eight months at best.

After that, the improvement becomes more and more minimal by the day. And that's for people half your age." She shrugged. "Truthfully, the pain may not be worth the possible results. I can't guarantee anything—except that if we don't continue our efforts, or for that matter if we fail in our efforts, your life will be altered permanently. You'll be no more than a dysfunctional three-stroke victim. I wish I could promise you success. I can't. Your age does not work in your favor. That's where we are now. It's your choice."

"You're telling me I've only got six months to have a shot at being half-assed normal?"

"No—I'm telling you that you *may* have a shot. And I don't care what a big shot you are, or think you are, Mr. Evans. The only person who can give you that shot is me."

She could probably tell what was going on in my mind, because I saw her eyes zeroing icily in on mine. "Make up your mind, because I don't like wasting my time. You're as complicated and difficult a case as I've handled in ten years. Frankly, you exhaust me. I'm breaking for a half hour to have a bite of lunch. That gives you half an hour to figure out which way you want to go.

"Oh, and by the way, we need to knock off the self-pity shit. It's as difficult for me to administer as it is for you to take it."

Was I a coward? Let's just say I was no hero. The thought of eight hours a day of physical, occupational, and speech therapy—learning how to walk heel-toe, heel-toe, the pain of getting my wooden fingers to metamorphose into human movement to pick up a fork, a knife, tie a shoelace, walk without falling—swirled around in my mind. One thing I knew, I did not want to be the Tin Man walking down the new millennium's Yellow Brick Road.

• • •

Forty minutes later, Tamara walked into the room and stood there beside me. "Well, at least now you know the deck you're holding. Which way do you want to play it?"

"I'm yours. No complaints." I looked into her eyes. "Pull off a miracle, will ya? Torture me good but get them limbs movin', my tongue waggin'." My eyes swelled. "Please."

Being kind, let's call the next six weeks blackout time. I kept saying to myself, *Move slow if you must, but don't stop.* And I didn't.

The Guy Upstairs must have been looking out for me.

By the end of the month, dexterous again was my tongue, deft my clarity, and an octave deeper my reborn voice. I couldn't make a fist yet, but my fingers were movin'. I couldn't bend my toes, but I could move them. Most important of all, my atrophied right limb was slowly getting into the rhythm of *heel-toe, heel-toe*, allowing me at least to *fake* a walk, with only a slight limp. I was on my way.

Then it happened. One day, while I was practicing heel-toeing it down my winding driveway, with Nurse Sosnick constantly critiquing my stride, I passed the tennis court. Something caught my eye, and I did a quick Evans double take. It completely disrupted my rhythm and landed me flat on my ass—and all the while, I was still looking at what had distracted me: the beautiful specimen out taking lessons from my old friend, tennis pro Darryl Goldman.

Something was stirring. I must be getting better!

Unable to take my eyes off her, I heel-toed it back to the court as she racketed her strokes with the grace and power of a pro, and the looks of an angel. As she lifted her head to serve, her eyes caught me watching. Without missing a beat, she dropped her racket and ran toward me.

It was Catherine Oxenberg. Strange: I had known her for some fifteen years, but we had hardly shared more than a hello during all that time. Though she was a total winner on every count, I had never given her a second thought. Always assumed she'd be too tough a challenge.

With the charm and thoughtfulness of an Audrey Hepburn, she embraced me as if we were long-lost lovers. Not only was she in touch with my illness, but she seemed genuinely concerned with my present health and future healing. An actress, yes, but my ego told me this was no performance. She exuded an intoxicating air, and a genuine desire to be there and help me in whatever way she could to ensure my road back to health.

Was my tumble a matter of timing? Certainly. But no girl had ever projected a more bewitching charm and fetching beauty than she. It was magic—for a fleeting moment, she made me feel like the man I was, not the man I *was*.

That afternoon, I visited Dr. Charles Kivowitz in his office, and I told him what happened. The good doctor got up from his chair and walked me into his private office. Was he smiling? No. He was concerned—deeply concerned.

"Bob, sit down and listen. You are not just a sick man. You are a very sick man. It was only six weeks ago that you were all but a dead man. If you'd been through successful open-heart surgery, you could well be on your way to a normal, healthy life. But that's not the case. You had a brain attack. Reoccurrence of a brain attack is not an uncommon thing. One minor jolt and

you're out—I mean *out*! It's not like the heart. You're not in condition physically, emotionally, or medically to even think about
getting involved in any kind of a relationship. You're allowing
your brain to act irrationally."

"Charlie," I interrupted, "I came down to tell you this, thinking you'd be pleased to see me high on life for the first time."

"You're not ready to feel high on life, Bob. You still don't understand this. Don't talk yourself into a quick fix. It could have
disastrous implications. This is not an exaggeration. I'd much
rather have seen you come in somber than hyper. Think of your
brain as a roller coaster—the higher it gets, the more speedy
and scary the fall. Take what I say seriously. I'm not asking you,
Bob. I'm telling you as your doctor. It's a must. That quick fix
could cost you a quick death."

He took me by the shoulders, turned me around so that our
eyes met.

"Please, Bob. I beg of you, take the slow road this time. It's
the difference between life and death."

Did I listen? Yes—for an hour.

When I got home, my first call was to Catherine. She was elated
to hear from me.

"Your voice is pure velvet, Evans."

"You make an old man feel mighty good."

"Old! Uh-uh. Age is only numbers!"

"Come over Friday. We'll watch *The Mask of Zorro*."

"How wonderful!" she purred. "I'm having some girlfriends
over for dinner. Can I invite them, too?"

"Of course." I would have said yes if she'd told me she was having twenty mutes.

That Friday evening, we sat next to each other with about eight or ten guests. Suddenly, I'm entertaining! Suddenly I'm telling stories! Suddenly I don't feel like going to bed! Suddenly I'm in love! Suddenly I'm on high.

Suddenly I'm doing everything Dr. Kivowitz said was wrong.

The week that followed was a mix of painful therapy and extraordinary therapy, Catherine being the latter. As we sat around, having a quiet dinner for two in the projection room, she opened her mouth and shocked the hell out of me.

"When I walked to the door that day and saw you standing there, my only thought was of death. You seemed to be dying. As you know, I'm into Eastern philosophy. I found my calling. I'm going to save you, heal you, bring you back to health."

"Dying? Did I look that bad?"

"No. I sensed death in the room."

How do you answer an offer like that? You don't! Instead, words came out of my mouth that would have given Dr. Kivowitz cardiac arrest.

"Marry me. Heal me. Save me."

She didn't say no, but she did say, "Isn't it a bit soon? Besides, even if I wanted to, I couldn't. I've been living with a man for the last four and a half years. He's terribly jealous; he's probably wondering where I am right now. And even if you were perfectly well, and I wasn't living with a man, I've never been married before. You'd be my first husband—and I'd be your fifth wife."

Both of us laughed, but I was on super-high—persuasive to the tens.

"Would we match up as the perfect couple on a computer dating service?" I asked. "Of course not. Just the thought of the two of us together would break the machine."

She quick-giggled.

"Funny? Yeah, but that's just the reason it works," I went on. "Are we conformists? You know and I know, both of us get off on breaking the rules. Is it impulsive? You bet your ass it is. But it's exciting. Look at you. You're as extraordinary and as beautiful as they make 'em, and you've been with this guy for four and a half years—and you're no further ahead in your life than you were the first day you met him.

"You're not happy, you can't be. I know it and you know it." She looked up at me without saying a word. "If you were, you'd have stopped me already."

She was listenin'. Mesmerized? Possibly. Shocked that I'd bull's-eyed her hidden frustrations? You bet your ass she was. Me? I was on an Evans roll.

"I'm also much too old for you. And, yes, you would be my fifth wife. Does it sound right? No way! Yeah, but it's just the reason it will work. If you really believe in Eastern philosophy the way you say you do, you have to embrace the fact that I'm really only nine weeks old. It was nine weeks ago, to the day, that I heard the fat lady sing. And here I am today, reborn."

A long silence.

"Lunch tomorrow." I half whispered.

She nodded her head yes.

14

Did I lie to Catherine? No! Quite the opposite. Every thought I spoke was genuine and totally true. Since I've been a kid, I've learned always to tell the truth. It has little to do with morality, but much to do with making one's bumpy road an easier one to drive.

Telling the truth gives you the luxury of never having to remember what you've said. At times it can cause a bit of friction, but that's a cheap price to pay for never having to wonder what you said in past encounters. The more complicated your life, the more important role truth plays. From body language to the spoken language, you're just more at ease with yourself, and it shows. I know.

Ah, but I ain't no saint. There's an asterisk to all this moral behavior.

On the Seine, escaping before
the husband returned, 1958.

With Ava Gardner and Tyrone Power on the set of *The Sun Also Rises*.

Surrounded by well-wishers after the premiere of *The Best of Everything* at New York's Paramount Theatre in New York, 1961.

With Norma Shearer,
who tapped me to play
her husband, at the
Beverly Hills Hotel.

With James Cagney
on the set of *Man of a
Thousand Faces*.

With Mia Farrow at her star wagon,
on the set of *Rosemary's Baby*.
Julian Wasser

Sue Mengers and Alain Delon at Woodland.

With Dick Van Patten, my friend since puberty and still going strong.

Alan Berliner

Entering the world premiere of *The Godfather* with my brother Charles,
Ali MacGraw, and then–Secretary of State Henry Kissinger.

With my longtime mentor
and friend Sidney Korshak.

My son, Joshua, and me, looking ahead to the future.

Ali, Joshua, and me, celebrating his twenty-first birthday at home.

My association with the Kennedy family continued through a close friendship with Teddy Kennedy. Here he is on one of his many visits to Woodland, post-tennis . . . pre-dinner.

Receiving the Golden Globe for Best Picture for *Chinatown* from one of the world's great femmes fatales, Catherine Deneuve.

Lunch with Dustin Hoffman and friends beneath my prized two-hundred-year-old California sycamore. Imagine . . . it stood here when the land was still owned by the Spanish crown.

With Jack Nicholson
and Roman Polanski,
sharing breakfast after
an all-nighter in Paris,
2005.

A great day for Jack,
1974.

*The Bruce Torrence Hollywood
Photograph Collection*

Nose-to-nose and heart-to-heart with Jack.

Catherine Oxenberg and me
on our wedding day.

With Barry Diller and Graydon Carter,
celebrating our prize at the Cannes Film Festival.

Charles Evans Jr.

With the dashing Graydon Carter and my two brilliant directors, Brett Morgen
and Nanette Burstein, arriving for a moment of triumph at the screening of
The Kid Stays in the Picture at the Cannes Film Festival.

Charles Evans Jr.

A great day: Reading the thumbs-up notices for *The Kid* documentary.

Sinisha Nisevie for Oliver Peoples

The book launch for *The Kid Stays in the Picture*
at Barneys New York in Beverly Hills.

Charles Evans Jr.

Omission ain't lying.

Call it a rationalization if you wish, but sometimes silence brings more to the table than words.

What I failed to tell dear Catherine was that I was on more drugs than I'd ever been on in my entire life. All legal, but all lethal. All with side effects when taken on their own. When you're cocktailing them with other legal lethals, the results are impossible to fathom.

Forget cocaine, heroin, ecstasy, acid. They're all illegal. With rare exception, they are all taken singularly. Dangerous, damaging, punishable? Certainly. But to compare any of the above to pharmaceutical cocktails is like comparing beer to tequila. Those medicinal cocktails have the potential to damage your every emotion, organ, and ounce of equilibrium. Their dangers can be more ruinous than the injury they're supposed to cure. It can take just one wrong ingredient in the mix to make Chinese torture feel like Shiatsu massage. The wrong combination can cause your rationality to go awry, your behavior to become incomprehensible, your bodily functions and movements to discombobulate.

Am I exaggerating its power? If anything, I'm underplaying it—unless you enjoy feeling like a time bomb.

At that moment, I'm thinking, *This cocktail must be working. I'm flying high.* Ideas of all kinds were bursting from my cerebellum: visions of films to make, books to write. And women to marry! Whether she realized it or not, Catherine was going to be my bride, sharing my adventures, creating our dreams.

Those drug cocktails were turning me into one dangerously delusional junkie.

• • •

Over grilled Chilean sea bass, corn on the cob, endive and tomato salad, and a feathery, balloon-shaped hot lemon soufflé, Catherine began to feel mighty comfortable behind them Woodland gates. I can't remember the things I spouted, but I had never in my entire life been more on my game at seducing another's mind.

When my major domo, Alan, brought in the lemon soufflé, I took a large spoon, scooped up the top, and put it to her mouth for her to taste.

"This reminds me of being in France," she purred.

With that, I took her hand. "Let's get out of here. I've got a surprise for you."

"But the soufflé . . ."

"That's just for openers."

"Where are we going?"

"If I told you, it wouldn't be a surprise."

My custom Jag convertible was awaiting us outside. "You drive, I'll direct."

"Why not?" She wide-smiled.

As we drove out she said, "How did you know this was my favorite car?"

"I didn't."

"It seems different from the others, though."

"It is. It was made for me, as a gift."

"You get nice gifts," she said.

Turning right on Lexington, I told her to make a left on Rodeo until we got to the north 300 block.

"It *must* have been custom-made," she said. "It drives like no other Jag I've ever been in."

"It's yours."

She started laughing. "Don't tease me, Bob. I couldn't take this from you. We hardly know each other."

"We know each other far better than you may think. This ain't no gift, Catherine. If you buy something for another, it's a gift. When you take something you cherish and give it to another, it's called sharing. Sharing is what love is all about."

"This is all too much, Bob. I don't know what to say."

"No, it's not. You've just underrated yourself for too long."

Hitting the 300 block on Rexford, I pointed to an open parking space. "Park your car over there."

Somewhat dazed, she parked the car. "Where to now, Mr. Evans?"

"Mr. Evans gets off on surprises."

We jaywalked across Rodeo and approached the gated door of Frances Klein Classic Jewels. Catherine knew the store all too well. As one of the proprietors was opening the gate, she grabbed my arm, looked up to me in total amazement, her face ashen.

"What are you doing?"

"It's not what I'm going to do. It's what you're going to do."

The proprietor had expected me. Catherine, trancelike, held my hand as we walked to the back of the store.

Without a word, the proprietor pulled out two velvet trays. In each compartment of each tray shined an antique diamond, emerald, ruby, and sapphire ring, each one boasting a distinguished provenance.

Looking up at the proprietor, she asked if he could give us a bit of privacy. He discreetly stepped away. Catherine looked at me sharply in the eye, whispering.

"Are you crazy?"

"Let me be the judge of that."

"I've known you less than a week. You've never even kissed me. I can't accept this from you. I've been living with a man for four and a half years."

"That's just the reason you *can* accept this from me. You've been living with this guy for four years, and you're no further ahead in your life, your career, your future than you were four years ago. Let's call it as it is. Instead of blossoming, you're standing still. You've got too much going for you. There's no girl on the screen who has your aplomb, style, beauty, and ability to boot. And where are you?"

Blankly, her eyes looked up, her ears taking in every syllable of every word.

"You're going backward. Because when you stand still, the only thing you get is older. Got it?"

Got it she did. On that day in July, no actor I know could have delivered those lines with more fervent conviction.

No actor I know could have been as drugged up as me, either.

I turned back to the open jewel trays. "Try none of them on, try all of them on, but take the one that hits your heart most."

As if she were under hypnosis, she tried on one ring after the other, then pointed to one on a tray that hadn't been taken from its case. The proprietor hastened to bring the tray forward and placed it in front of Catherine.

It was obvious. One ring stood Michael Jordan–tall over all the others.

Putting it on, she looked at it for a long moment. "Isn't it extraordinary?"

Jule Styne wasn't wrong. Diamonds are a girl's best friend.

Finally, looking at the ring, I nonchalantly whispered, "It's yours. Let's get out of here." Without even asking the cost, I slipped the ring on the fourth finger of her left hand and we left. My doctors could've been right. I didn't give a fuck. I was in love.

On the way back to the car, I had a bit of trouble walking—a problem I hadn't told her about. She had a little trouble as well, but for different reasons. She didn't know what planet she was on.

I opened the driver's-side door for her with all the aplomb I could muster. "My lady, drive us home."

I didn't have to tell her—she knew the way. And she knew what I meant by *home*.

On the way there, she tried to process what was happening. "Bob, I can't take this ring from you," she said. "I'm living with a man. What'll I tell him when I get back to our home? What'll I tell my daughter, India?"

"Show your daughter both of your rings—the ring you've been wearing the last four years, and the ring you're wearing as of today. Sometimes a child's instincts are better than an adult's. Ask her which promises a brighter future for her mother. And whatever happens, happens. What time does your guy get home?"

"About eight."

"This is going to be resolved tonight, Catherine. I am not crazy." I was, of course. "Impulsive, yes. Lucky to have met you—yes, yes. In love with you—more than any guy you've ever known. And for a damned good reason. I told you I'm only nine weeks old. I'm starting a new life with the most extraordinary lady I've ever met. Do I look forward to making her blossom in the way she deserves?

"Catherine, I'm not being altruistic. I am being selfish. The more you blossom, the more you succeed, the happier my new life will be. Together we'll make them dreams come true. Is it a risk? Sounds like it—but it's not. It's spiritual in the purest sense. Much stronger than lust. Much stronger, even, than love. We've touched something neither of us will touch again. That's why I'm not going to allow anyone to talk me out of this. I'm not going to allow anyone to dissuade you.

"It's four o'clock on Tuesday afternoon, Catherine. I'm not going to ask you to handle your domestic problem today—"

"Strange how fate is," she interrupted as she pulled into the courtyard. "John happens to be leaving Thursday for a four-day weekend in Las Vegas."

"What does that tell you?"

For the first time she looked lovingly into my eyes. "That it's right."

"I shan't even kiss you, Catherine. The first time I'm going to kiss you is when you are Mrs. Evans. How exciting that is— wanting you as much as I do, yet not wanting to touch you. I feel so blessed, Catherine. Our vows will be an experience we'll both always remember."

I said enough—no, more than enough. Now I wanted her to take her new car, go back to her old house, show her daughter her new shining light, and wait by the phone to see if my audition got me the part.

I got out of the car. "Go back and see your kid. Tell her every-thing. Sunday at eleven, while your boyfriend's shooting craps in Vegas, we'll become one, and off we'll travel to the south of France with India and her nanny."

As if in a trance, without saying another word to me, she pulled her car around and disappeared toward the gates that led out of Woodland to the outside world. Me, I'm bettin' that the outside world couldn't feel as good as the inside did.

I fell on my bed, exhausted but exhilarated. Was I high? Like I'd never been before. Was I on drugs? Like I'd never been before.

I opened the packet of my pharmaceutical goodies, added two Valiums, took my blood pressure. It was 180 over 110. Fuck it. If I die, I die. It was worth the afternoon. Never gave a better performance. It was easy—I meant it.

Now I just had to lie there and wait to see if I got the part.

I told my staff, "I'm shutting off the phones. I'm out to every-body, no matter who it is, except Catherine Oxenberg. As soon as she calls, and it should be before eight, buzz me on the inter-com."

She had three and a half hours to speak to her daughter, make up her mind, and get rid of the guy. Me, I'm just lyin' and waitin'.

I knew the new Jag she was driving would start some kind of conversation when her guy walked in. Not to mention the rock on her finger. But I also knew I wasn't smart enough to read a woman's mind. I tried to watch the five o'clock news. I couldn't. Six o'clock news, same thing. I just closed my eyes and listened to the sound of the fountains surrounding my home.

By seven o'clock, my confidence began to waver. I'd had it

happen before: great audition, but I came in second. Someone else got the part. Coming in second ain't no fun, no matter what you're up for.

At 7:22, the intercom buzzed. In his most pristine English, Alan announced: "Mr. Evans, Miss Oxenberg is on the phone."

Fear shot through me as if I'd stepped on the third rail of the IRT. For that split second, I was totally at a loss.

With the coolness of a blackjack dealer in Vegas, she uttered, "John is leaving tomorrow morning. So why confront him? India loves my new shining light. So do I. Are we still on for Sunday?"

"At eleven."

"I'll arrange the preacher. Your luck hasn't been too good in the past. See you, darling, tomorrow."

My first thought was, *Now what? Do I tell my son? Do I call my lawyers? Do I speak to my doctor? Whoever I tell will want to lock me up.*

Coincidentally, my son Joshua came over to visit me that night. To say he was shocked, angry, suspicious, and concerned for my sanity would be an underplay.

I stood my ground. "I'm meeting with my lawyers tomorrow. My entire trust will be left to you. You know, kid? It feels good to be alive. And hey, Joshua, don't I deserve one of them big smiles before I take my hike?"

He left on good terms, agreeing that we'd talk some more in the days to come. And the days were few—four, to be exact. But my concern over his negative reaction was put to rest, at least as far as I was concerned. I understood where he was coming from, but more important, he understood where I was coming from. At ten the next morning, I called two of my attorneys to my home at four o'clock with my will and a notary public. Both of them asked why. Both of them got the same answer: "Don't ask. You don't wanna know."

Before too long, the Next Mrs. Evans was on the horn. "Can I come over? I'm so excited." She had told her two best girlfriends about her impending first marriage, and they embraced it as if she were marrying Baron David Rothschild. I'm thinking, *Either you're lying to me, or they're crazy, too.*

She arrived an hour later, for the first time bringing her daughter, India. Catherine showed her around her new digs, then brought her into my projection room and introduced her to her new stepfather.

"Nice to meet you, Mr. Evans." I wasn't going to have her call me Daddy!

Catherine took India's hand and walked her out to the tennis court. "We'll be taking tennis lessons three times a week from Darryl. Isn't that wonderful?"

A silence. Didn't like it. Didn't blame the kid, either.

They went for a tour of the house. Ten minutes later, Catherine buzzed me from the intercom. "India and I are leaving. We'll see you tonight for din-din. I invited some of my girlfriends over to join us watching *Entrapment*, if that's all right with you."

"Hope India's coming."

"Oh, she'll be with me."

When I saw my attorneys that afternoon, they didn't know which psychiatrist to call first. But my resolve was so stern that they had little choice but to follow my orders.

That night, Catherine, her eight girlfriends, and her daughter, India, came by for the screening of *Entrapment*. Her friends all seemed to embrace our coming nuptial bliss. The clock was ticking.

Then, as I was walking her to our outdoor Jacuzzi, India looked up at me. "You know, Mr. Evans, you remind me so much of my grandfather. Do you know him?"

The terrible thing was, I did!

How is it that one line uttered by one person can blow euphoria into depression? India had said it all in that one line. I could have bought her Disneyland and it wouldn't have changed her feelings.

God, did I age quickly that night!

We all loved the picture. Afterward, though, I was scared to get up from my chair. My legs felt like the Tin Man's. My afternoon pills were wearing off, and I needed a new batch to keep me from turning into Dorian Gray. As far as Catherine and the rest were concerned, I wasn't just on the road to recovery—I had recovered. And one thing I couldn't show was my hand—that is, my legs.

Cristal flowed like ginger ale, except for me and India. She was too young to drink it; I was too old. But I faked it good.

With the pristine manners of the countess she was, Catherine announced to one and all that our impending marriage would take place at eleven o'clock Sunday—beneath our tree.

I started laughing. "Who's marrying us—our butler?"

"Darling, that's all taken care of."

"Thanks for telling me."

"I told you, that part was my assignment. I got her out of the Yellow Pages."

"The Yellow Pages?"

"That's right, 1-800-I-MARRY-U. When I called, Dr. Patricia Swanson said, 'Thank you for calling the marriage line, dearly beloved.' I felt immediately comfortable. My intuition told me Dr. Swanson was the right person. Didn't make one other call."

Before I could answer, she said, "Evans, don't question my judgment on this. You're batting zero for four—don't forget it."

"Forget it? I'm looking forward to it."

On Friday morning, I paid a visit to Dr. Charlie Kivowitz, the captain of the medical team that was keeping me breathing. When I told him I was getting married on Sunday—and to whom—his face paled. He sat down silently to think; I could see his hands shaking.

"Bob, I don't think you understand one thing," he finally said. "Only a month ago, your limbs weren't moving, you couldn't talk, your blood pressure was a roller coaster at best, and—most important—your brain was swollen. It still is. This isn't a crap game. You've had therapists by your side twenty-four hours a day. But it's worse than that. I'm starting to think the stroke has really affected your judgment. You're fucking crazy. Does Catherine have any idea how sick you are?"

I didn't answer.

He stood up. "Well? Tell me. Does she know how sick you are?"

"It's a tough question to answer, Doctor."

"No, it isn't. Because if she knows how sick you are and she marries you, she's just as sick as you are."

"Hey! Hold it, Charlie. I haven't been showing you all my

cards. She knows all about my stroke. As a matter of fact, we joke about it. I tell her I'm nine weeks old."

The doctor didn't laugh. "You're not nine weeks old. And if you get married, you won't live another nine weeks. You need nurses and therapists, not a wife and a child running around the house. I'm calling Catherine now."

I grabbed the phone from the doctor's hand.

"Don't call her, Charlie, please."

I thought, *He's a fucking doctor. He's just trying to scare the shit out of me. Fuck him and his medical diplomas. I'm going to get to the church on time, and he ain't gonna stop me.*

The doctor started laughing. "You were putting me on, weren't you, Evans?"

I smiled back. "Well, sort of."

"It wasn't funny."

I had to switch gears quick to get out of his office a free man. "I'm a better actor than you thought, Charlie. I met her on the tennis court. We had some fun, that's all."

"How long have you known her?"

"A couple of weeks."

"Bob, please. These last two months with you have been exhausting, to put it mildly. You know, doctors are human. We carry stress, too. You're walking a very thin line, Bob. Don't take it lightly. Promise me?"

"Ah, come on, Charlie. You can't take a joke."

"You're right. I'm not here to hear your jokes. I'm here to keep you alive. Don't forget that."

"I'm sorry, I'm sorry. Won't do it again, I promise. See you on Tuesday." After the elevator door closed, I said, "Your ass, I'll see you on Tuesday. I'll be in the south of France by then."

Would you say those pharmaceuticals I was taking were fucking with my head?

Later that day, my dear bride started moving her things into her new domicile.

It was Saturday. I was lying on my bed. Catherine, India, her nanny, and I were booked on a plane to leave for Nice the next day. And my blood pressure was 195 over 110—even with the help of all those pills.

With my blood pressure hitting them numbers, I had two other doctor friends over. Robert Siegel advised me that taking an eleven-hour plane flight would be playing Russian roulette. I wasn't afraid of dying, but I didn't want to die on a German plane. They contacted a stroke center near Hotel du Cap, to keep them on alert. But after further persuasion, I was convinced it could be more than a bumpy ride—rather, a final one.

By this time, Catherine was all prepared to leave for the south of France. How could I tell her I was a prime candidate for another stroke? When she got back from the fitting for her bridal gown, she found me still sitting with the two doctors. I played it out as though I had a sinus condition.

"I checked the weather conditions in Nice," I told her. "It's pouring there and they're expecting a big storm to come in. A long fuckin' flight, anyway. Let's make it easier, go someplace where we can get home quicker, get things set up properly."

What a trouper! It didn't bother her one iota. "If you're not up to it, darling, let's stay closer to home."

Well, let's just say Montecito ain't Antibes and Santa Ynez ain't the Hotel du Cap.

Saturday night. I'm thinking, *The less I see her before the wedding, the better my chances of closing the deal.* That night, she and her girlfriends went out to the Palm to celebrate the secret tying of the knot. The next morning, Alan left early to collect Dr. Swanson, who would be performing the ceremony at noon.

Dr. Swanson, as it happened, lived in Pasadena. Was she the real thing? You bet. Did she have all the right credentials? Yes. When Alan picked her up, the figure he encountered was that of a conservative English lady. But she had one idiosyncratic quirk: Between Pasadena and Beverly Hills, she nonchalantly described her only roommate, her English bulldog—who she believed was the reincarnation of her deceased husband.

Why Alan didn't grab me by the arm and tell me this earlier I'll never know. Maybe he thought it was normal. In actuality, it wasn't any less normal than the proceedings that followed.

Catherine never looked more beautiful. And our wedding was like an acid trip: colorful, absurd, and, yes, unreal. The bride, ravishing. The groom, ravished. One part of my brain was telling me how lucky I was. The other was asking, *What do I do next?*

It happened to be the hottest day of the summer, with the temperature hitting the century mark. Me, I felt like I was, too. I was just hoping to stand long enough to say, "I do." With my legs wobblin', I barely got the two words out. A married man I was.

The guests congratulated the bride, all fifty of them. Did they mean it? Of course not. Did they think ours was a match made in Heaven? More like a scene from Fellini.

A little later, we departed for the Santa Ynez Inn in two limousines: Catherine and I in one; India, her nanny, Catherine's closest friend, and her daughter in the other. When we finally arrived at the honeymoon suite, though, I could barely get out of the car.

Catching my breath, I grabbed the door to prevent myself from falling. I was an odds-on favorite to pass out right there in front of the suite of bliss.

Catherine caught on quick. "Darling, it's so hot out. Let me help you up the stairs."

"No, I'm fine." But she knew different.

Did I carry Catherine over the threshold? Not quite. It would have been easier for her to carry me. Her female instincts came into play as she slowly guided me to the king-sized honeymoon bed, my head spinning all the while. Poor Catherine, she'd waited all these years to be a bride, and she sure in hell didn't wind up with Rubirosa.

Later that night, she fixed me a bubble bath in a sunken tub. When it came to getting out, I couldn't move. With all her strength, she grabbed both my arms and helped me out. For an instant, I felt as if I were back in the rehab ward at Cedars. Not a great way to start off a romantic melding. At that moment, we both knew: This was a far cry from a kiss to build to a dream on.

I lay awake until the sun came up, thinking, *How unfair to the lady beside me. Her first marriage and she ends up with a cripple. Worse than that, a fraud who claimed he was fit, who, in reality, was a fake.*

My guilt turned to paranoia. Catherine, to her credit, didn't show her hand. In some way, she was determined to try to make it work. Whether it was the drugs, the guilt, or my total disillusionment at the shape I was in, I became pensive, silent, and scared.

The next morning, Catherine and her entourage made their way up the hill to the pool and gym. As soon as they left, I got up, moved to the terrace, and started my walking exercises: *Heel, toe, heel, toe.* Taking a deep breath and crossing my fingers I started the trek up the hill to join them.

Damn it, I couldn't make it.

Halfway there, I sat down on a rock near the road. The hill wasn't steep, but it mattered little. Not only was I out of breath, but that damn *heel, toe* wasn't working. I was on full limp.

I started to cry. Kivowitz was right. Married less than a day and I'm falling apart.

Pull yourself together, Evans. You've made tougher treks.

The truth is, I hadn't. Call it dealing with half a deck. Call it what you want, but I knew I wasn't up for the role.

Before I hit the pool, I sat down, caught my breath, then put on my best smile and strode in. The four of them were in the gym. I couldn't join them on the treadmill, but at least I could swim. Luckily, they weren't watching. I made the length of the pool— and that was it. Out of breath and dizzy, not wanting to show what bad shape I was in, I opened the gym door and shouted, "Meet you back at the cottage!"

The minute I began my descent, though, I felt off balance. I knew only one thing: I could not afford to fall. When one of the housekeepers passed by a moment later, I stopped her and asked, "Please walk me down to the cottage. Hold me tight."

Desperate to conceal my inadequacies, I willed myself to be up for the night. Catherine was an angel. She cared, caressed, and soothed me. A better actress than I thought, but I didn't care. At least it was an embrace—a needed one.

Without saying a word, she said it all. My cavalier attitude, my misguided play for a quick fix, had shattered the dreams of this extraordinary lady lying beside me.

Finally, pragmatism prevailed over promises. Painful, yes, but pretending ain't never been my game. I had coerced her to be my bride under pretenses that were all but delusional. The good doctor was right, that quick fix wasn't the answer. Sadly, a quick good-bye was.

I took her in my arms. With my forefinger under her chin, I lifted her head, met her eyes.

"I did you wrong, kid. Thought I could handle it, but my feet ain't big enough to fill them shoes. How can I be a father to India, think of us having another kid, when I can't even get out of a bathtub without your help?"

She knew it. I knew it. It was over and out. Hello and good-bye.

By the time the limousine got back to Woodland, all of Catherine's possessions had been removed and back at her pad a half mile away. She would have everything cozy, as if nothing had happened—a hot bubble bath, a favorite dinner . . . chicken in the pot . . . served in bed—by the time her four-year live-in got back from Vegas.

Her weekend lark? What lark? Just married and divorced, that's all.

Guys are so dumb. Feather his ego, give him the best fuck he's had in years, and any man will pass out like the stud he thinks he is, not the spud he really is.

Could've pulled it off, too. Yeah, but she would have had to have married Mr. Anonymous rather than Mr. Infamous, giving them newspaper Fourth Estaters a field day. The real joke, however, was on them. While those mongers were still salaciously summarizing our betrothal, we were standing in front of the annulment man.

Sadie, Sadie, married lady, no loner was she.

Ah, but single she was thrilled to be . . .

. . . all because of me.

That was then; this is now. No heir to Valentino—rather, an over-the-hill lothario limping down the beach alone. Uselessness and loneliness permeated my every thought. The tentacles of agoraphobia already had me in their grip. Paranoia seeped into my thoughts, making me realize I had two choices: I could fall into a life of self-pity, or I could Popeye it: *Hey, I yam what I yam and that's all that I am.* Fuck 'em, fuck 'em all.

Standing there barefoot as the last of the ocean's ripples washed past my ankles, I beheld God's Church of Nature. In its purest sense, I had finally found religion.

I looked up at the Almighty. My eyes teared.

"Help me, O God," I cried. "I will not be a victim. Help me. *Please* help me."

Passing onlookers walked nearby, afraid to get too close. One thing they did know: This was one crazy cat! Ah, but they were wrong. This was one blessed cat. As the sun made its descent, I made my ascent. My agoraphobia waned, my stride wavered less, paranoia slipped from my view.

Then, all at once, a fiery orange full moon filled up the sky like a second sun. Could it be the Man Upstairs had heard my plea? The heat of the moon's fire was voice enough. No matter how cold the world out there might be, for the first time since I'd faced the white light and heard the Fat Lady, I felt the strength only He could have given me.

Do I believe in miracles? You bet your ass I do!

Back to Woodland I traveled. As I entered my onetime Land of Oz, I was totally alone . . . yet not alone at all. I was surrounded by a 360-degree vista of every kind of tree imaginable: a sea of hundreds of polychromatic rosebushes, gardenias, lemon and lime trees, evergreens, and eucalyptus trees, many reaching two hundred feet or more. Not for nothing was our little street called Woodland.

At last, I felt protected by my roots of thirty years.

Wandering through my Garden of Eden, I lay down on the grass beneath the sprawling, two-hundred-year-old sycamore behind my house. For more than an hour, my eyes panned the vistas I had once taken for granted. It may have been the first time I lay behind the gates of my Garden of Eden alone. "Am I really here?" I wondered aloud. And that prompted my first call to the outside world.

I dialed Warren, my seven-digit pal. "It's Evans. Before you get a chance to play Mr. District Attorney, don't ask me any questions. Get Jack and come down, will ya? I need ya. I need ya bad."

Couldn't have been more than ten or twelve minutes before the Two Musketeers showed up at Woodland. They must have known I meant it.

"Well, you got yourself a new name," I said.

Warren didn't laugh. Jack did. "Yeah?" Warren said.

"Quick Draw!"

Jack interrupted. "Good name, Pro."

Beatty continued. "When it comes to time to celebrate, you sure keep it a secret."

"Don't you?"

"Yeah, but I can get away with it. You can't."

"Thanks a lot."

Nicholson cackled. "That's why he's called the Pro."

"Did you come here just to make me feel bad?"

They chuckled. Twenty-one marriages of all faiths had been consecrated under the languid branches of that old sycamore. It was known as the Lucky Tree. Nineteen were still in play. The only two that took a dive? Mine.

Beatty gave it to me again, below the belt.

"You're dumber than I thought, Evans. Why the fuck didn't you call me? I would have tied your hands behind your back, put tape over your mouth. I've known her for years. She's wonderful, but she's not for you."

"You've known everybody for years!"

"You were just afraid of a bad report, huh?" We both knew he was right.

Nicholson just laughed. "When you need me, Keed, I'm there

for you faster than a rabbit fucks. When it gets to hitchin' time, though, I ain't even invited. Instead I'm lying out on the sundeck, holding my dick with one hand and fielding calls with the other. 'Who did he marry? Where'd he get married?' And I just laughed. 'I know nothing about it.' Next time you're in deep, Irish is out of town. Call nine-one-one."

"You're right, Irish. So are you, you prick," I said, looking at Warren. "I was scared. Know why? I knew you would have talked me out of it. Got a flash for you. While we're laughin', Cinderella's at her fuckin' attorney's, gettin' an annulment."

The two of them looked at each other. Nicholson gaped. "After four days?"

"You're wrong. After two. My own doctor told me I was certifiable."

The DA turned on me. "Certifiable? Are you kidding me? That's brilliant! How many guys can sweep a girl off her feet, take her away from a guy she was engaged to for four years, marry her, and dump her in one week?"

Jack interrupted again. "The best part?" His eyebrows arching north: "He did it with half a tongue!"

They both burst out laughing. "Now that's talent!"

I awakened the next morning realizing that there was one thing I'd yearned for, one luxury that had eluded me, all my life: POM—peace of mind.

Many a friend called, wanting to drop by. Despite my waterside epiphany, I wasn't up for the part. I was becoming more and more reclusive by the day.

At the behest of Warren and Jack, I paid my first visit ever to a psychopharmacologist. After two hours of heavy analysis, he demanded that I go on antidepressants immediately. He would brook no objections.

"Take advantage of our latest breakthroughs; they'll work for you. I urge you to treat this with the same seriousness with which you treated your strokes. Left untreated, this condition could cause a . . . critical setback." I got the hint.

As I waited for the elevator on my way out of his office, I all but broke down. The doors opened . . . and there stood a blast from the past, whose presence in my life remained as potent today as it had decades ago. Yet she had no idea who I was. Could I have changed that much?

It was the winter of 1963. I was in my apartment in New York, taking a bath, when the phone rang.

"Roberto, you must come to dinner tonight so I can introduce you to the next Mrs. Evans. She's possibly the most beautiful woman I've ever met . . . and she's all alone. Doesn't know anyone in town."

"Where and when?"

Only one man on earth could have lured me with a pitch like that. Porfirio Rubirosa.

He was a woman's man, a man's man, a modest man, a gentleman, and widely chronicled as the greatest cocksman of the twentieth century. So legendary was his endowment that "How's your Rubirosa?" became worldwide slang. Marilyn Monroe, Ava Gardner, Kim Novak, Jayne Mansfield, Eva Perón—they all waited in line to find out.

Privately, he confirmed one story: An obnoxious drunk stood by Rubi at the urinal in the men's room of the Ritz hotel in Paris. "How big does that son of a bitch get when it's hard?" the drunk asked, nudging him. Bored from decades of being asked the same question, he nonchalantly answered: "I don't really know. It takes so much blood to get it up, I always pass out!"

Known to many as "Rubi"—to some, less elegantly, as "Rub-ber Hosa"—in less than a decade he pulled off the nuptial par-lay of the century by marrying the two richest women in the world: Doris Duke, heiress to the Duke tobacco fortune, and Barbara Hutton, heiress to the Woolworth dime store fortune. He married them, divorced them, and left them fanatically jeal-ous of each other.

No one could claim even a distant second to Rubirosa's Throne of Seduction. But he was more than that. An airplane pilot, a daring two-goal handicap polo player, a title-holding sports car racer, tournament tennis player, and a boxer to boot. He had a full-scale boxing ring in his chalet outside Paris—not for show, but for the three competitive rounds he put in each day. I know, I was his houseguest more than once—and I was never able to lift my arms for the third round.

I had been introduced to him at my bogus engagement party in Paris, and that one moment almost made up for my disastrous trip. We became instant pals. Macho and mysterious, Rubi was the only guy I've ever known who attracted the attention of men as fervently as women. Hosting Rubi for dinner brought even the most reclusive potential guests to the table. He was one fuckin' stellar attraction! Ever modest, he often whispered to me, "I'm sure you're wrong, Bob. She wouldn't want anything to do with me. I'm much too old for her."

"Sure, Rubi! You know different, I know different. Next!"

He lived by his own rules, constantly mocking himself, laugh-ing about his inability to lead a structured life. Money, or lack of it, never bothered him. Why should it? It was always there for the asking.

As we were leaving a boring lunch together in New York, he asked me what he thought was a serious question. "Roberto, why is it the ambition of most men to save money, and mine is to spend it?"

"They ain't Rubi, that's why!"

He knew where I was coming from. He also knew I was right.

In the winter of 1962, we four-engined it to Palm Beach to attend their event of the year, the International Red Cross Ball. From around the world they flew—Cary Grant, Yul Brynner, Kirk Douglas—filling the gala with movie stars galore.

Walking in with Rubi that evening was nothing less than mind-boggling. The movie stars became instant background. From debu-tramps to royalty, every eye in the joint turned to Rubi—and then, by reflex, to his crotch. Me? I was embarrassed. Him? No way. He was used to it. That was his legend. Even if he wanted to, as he often said, he couldn't shake it!

A few months later, Rubi was in New York with his wife of five years, Odile Rodin. She was his fifth and last, the only one who wasn't extraordinarily wealthy or famous. Oh, but she was extraordinarily beautiful. He had met and married her when she was only nineteen, a young actress on an express train to success as a French femme fatale. She quickly changed her mind.

Two hours later, we were all having dinner at La Cote Basque. The girl I was with hardly spoke a word of English; my Portuguese was even worse. It didn't matter. I was in love. This five-eleven, raven-haired Brazilian beauty was a knockout! I was the only one of the four who couldn't converse in Portuguese. She charmingly insisted that we all speak English. Continually making fun of herself, she didn't give up trying. Her name? Florinda

Bolkan. To my surprise, she was the reigning Glamor Queen of Brazilian flicks.

Her insistence on trying to speak English led my ego to believe she really dug me. What a hot gift on a cold night, I thought. Possibly Rubi's right. The next Mrs. Evans. Better we don't break the language barrier—it'll last longer.

After the soufflés, Rubi suggested we try out Le Club, a private disco that had just opened not too far away. Though the weather was bitter cold, we took off on foot. No matter the weather, Rubi never sported a topcoat. Me? I felt the warmth of Heaven.

"Florinda Evans. Sounds good," I repeated to myself as we entered the club. Perfect, I thought. My Latin dancin' will get to her big!

We danced till we were drenched in sweat. "I'll drop you off at the hotel with the Rubirosas," I whispered to her. "Wait a half hour, then I'll come back and pick you up." How fetching her smile as we danced as one to the beat of the tango.

Exhausted, we gave up the floor for our chairs at the table. Odile leaned forward. Her hand crossed Rubi's, then grabbed mine, shocking me like I'd never been shocked before. Looking straight into my eyes, she whispered, with the coldness of a prosecuting attorney, four words that severed my every dream of Florinda.

"Forget her. She's mine!"

Moments later, the four of us made our departure. Rubi suggested we walk back to the St. Regis, just a short distance away. As naturally as two people dancing, Odile and Florinda walked arm in arm up the block toward First Avenue. Their two men trailed a couple of yards. Me? I'm going nuts: An hour ago, Florinda was the next Mrs. Evans. Now she's dyking it with Mrs. Rubirosa.

"Well, it doesn't play like she's going to be the next Mrs. Evans," I muttered.

"You never know, Robert . . ."

"I do know. Odile just gave me the layout."

Rubi laughed. "Roberto, you don't know Brazilian women. She told me you are the first man she wants to meet in New York. Your picture is showing in Brazil now. Down there, they call you the Latin Lover. Maybe you should move there. She called Florinda after finishing her last picture and said she couldn't wait to meet us in New York and firecrack the city. And Roberto, the first person she wanted to meet was you—the bullfighter. That's what they call you down there. That's why I called you as soon as I checked into the hotel, Odile says, 'Call Roberto! Call Roberto!'"

With the graciousness of his Latin manners, he opened his arms. "Roberto, Brazilian women—they are the best. Look at them. Can't you see?"

"Sure, sure. It's the three of you and me. I'm the beard."

"Beard? She wants a big romance in New York!"

"You mean between you, Odile, and Florinda? And me? I hop a cab and go home with the morning papers."

He laughed. "Roberto, you must understand. Brazil is a country of love."

"Can we change shoes? So, she's not the next Mrs. Evans. Can I at least be a fly on the wall?"

"My shoes? They won't help you. They won't let *me* be one." Rubi turned serious. "Roberto, there's as much a chance of

Odile letting me get close to Florinda as there is for me to re-marry Doris again."

"Rubi, are you saying . . . ?"

"No! Odile won't even let me watch!"

The light changed and we made our way across the street in silence. I started to laugh. "Rubi, Odile's no fool. If I were her, there's not a shot in hell I'd let you be in the same room with Florinda."

The Master smiled, knowing his legend all too well. "Roberto, that's the price I've had to pay," he whispered.

"After putting me through tonight, you owe me a big one," I told him. "And it's a *must*."

"Whatever you want, Roberto. Anything."

Taking out a pen and paper, I wrote down a name and number and handed it to him. "First thing tomorrow, make a date for four and have this guy as a filler instead of me, will ya? Give Florinda the same buildup you gave to me. Make it a repeat performance of this evening." I smiled. "That's all I ask."

"Warren?" Rubi laughed. "Florinda doesn't know who Warren Beatty is."

Apparently, Florinda wasn't that faithful. She went on to become the Countess Marina Cicogna's live-in girlfriend. By coincidence, the countess, one of Italy's wealthiest, was also one of Italy's most prestigious film producers. In time, it was easier getting a date to see the pope than it was to pull Florinda away from the countess.

I did get married, though. Not to Florinda, but rather to Camilla Sparv, a sensational Swede. We spent our honeymoon as guests of guess who? The Rubirosas. At Spain's most royal resort: the Marbella Beach Club.

For two weeks, in July 1964, the four of us were inseparable. The only problem was Rubi's continued insistence on picking up every check.

"Rubi, I'm not a charity case."

"Ah, but Roberto, I am the best man. I'll have it no other way!"

Seeing Camilla fixate on Rubi's endowment, I couldn't help thinking, *Can't disagree, Rubi. You are the best man.*

The morning after a night of awesome fireworks over the waters of Marbella, Rubi insisted we travel by car to a small town in Spain.

The road, bumpy. The thermometer, tipping one hundred. Yeah, but Rubi's ebullience was on high. Me? I didn't know what the fuck was going on. We arrived at an ancient town. "Roberto, I take you here to offer you my gift of marriage to Camilla. We are now entering Ronda," he pointed to a bullring. "It is the oldest bullring in the world."

As we drove through the old town he pointed to the bullring. "It is the heritage of Ronda's township. We go there now!" Smiling, "Within the corrida, my wedding gift awaits you!"

Nonplussed, Camilla and I followed Rubi and Odile into the ancient corrida. There, the most romantic gift of my life, one that no money could buy, one that only Rubi could arrange, awaited us. Dressed to the tens in their "suit of lights" were the two most legendary matadors in Spanish history: Luis Dominguin and Antonio Ordóñez. The two men were all but godly to the Latin peoples of the world—but both looked up to Rubi as though he were the godly one. To fulfill his wish, they performed mano a mano, each fighting a bull in honor of my marriage with Camilla.

They did it for Rubi. He did it for me.

Exactly one year later, on July 5, 1965, Rubi's powerful Ferrari sports car jumped the curb and crashed into a tree in Paris. He died in the ambulance on the way to the hospital. The wooden steering wheel—the type used in racing competition—had crushed his chest. At fifty-six, he died the way he lived: moving fast!

My luck, the week of my annulment was a quiet week for dirt. No scandals, infidelities, thefts, or cases of treason. My dirt became the perfect headline-filler. All the wire services, radio and TV gossip shows, the magazines and newspapers coast to coast, from A to Z, made my forty-eight-hour betrothal number one on their hit list. This was the real thing: fact that reads like bad fiction. Makes for prime gossip every time, pal.

Not a fiction writer worth his weight would have had the gall to invent the nuptial union of our little bombshell: *The Countess and the Philanderer Tie the Knot*. Named for her ancestress, Catherine the Great of Russia, related to the House of Windsor, the daughter of HRH Princess Elizabeth of Yugoslavia and the granddaughter of the Regent King of Yugoslavia, Catherine Oxenberg's dazzling beauty and royal pedigree pedestaled her a potential jewel for most every crown in the world. After studying privately for years with Richard Burton, she heard the beckoning call of Hollywood. Not stepping out of character, she portrayed Princess Diana twice: in *The Royal Romance of Charles and Diana* in 1982, and ten years later in *Charles and Diana: Unhappily Ever After.* What better casting, both personally and professionally: Catherine was the real thing!

Yeah, but I was the real thing, too. Internationally notorious, a womanizer to a fault, I had had four previous marriages, and they lasted less than seven years in total. Everyone who heard the news had the same reaction: "I don't believe it!"

Being the subject of gossip most of my adult life taught me that, no matter what the gossip, without an utterance from its principals it's a four- or five-day stampede. After that, the press heads on to other shores to dig up fresher dirt. Knowing Catherine, she would be impossible to find. She had too many places to hide.

That made me the target of their poison pens.

The one place I knew they wouldn't think they could find me was lying in my bed. Well, that's just where I assembled my staff.

I gave it to them straight. "Woodland, as of this moment, is under quarantine. It's zippered lips and bulging pockets time—and that fits all. All phones are off. Every gate goes on double lock. If a mole gets through, you've failed. There's no trespassing, no deliveries, no calls. Got it? For the next few days, Woodland's a tomb. Not a foot enters, not a foot leaves."

Having laid down the law, I laid out a little incentive for enforcement. "It's also 'get rich' time. Total adherence, each quarantined day, puts five Ben Franklins in your pockets. Know this clearly: A mistake by one is a washout for all. I'm looking for a short quarantine; you should be looking for a long one. This is the single most important assignment of your careers. Only one thing that must be accomplished: From this moment on, I am the Shadow. Any questions?"

Though our pictures ran in most every paper and magazine across the country, not one of them motherfuckers could get a single firsthand quote on the story. That would have been their passport to a continuing saga. Without it, in time something else would come along and distract them.

It sure as hell did. As my public laceration reached its height, President Bill Clinton stepped in to save the day—by giving the world his deposition detailing his tryst with Monica Lewinsky. Every last salacious innuendo was included, including the meaning of the word *is*.

Me? The timing made me savor the moment. What a luxury it was to be yesterday's news! Now you see me, now you don't.

That was the way I wanted it to be forever.

It didn't quite work out that way.

My euphoria over my newfound anonymity caused me to extend my quarantine for another three days. Once it was lifted, I gave my staff two days off, filled their pockets with green . . . and asked them to leave my phones off. How romantic those days alone—total silence, and the extra kick of knowing I'd beat the Fourth Estate at their own game. Sad to say, but I can't remember a more romantic three days in bed.

Ring-ring-ring went the phone. On the other end? An undeniable request. Sumner Redstone's seventy-fifth birthday party. I couldn't say no.

In steps English. "Sir, if am to get you to the church on time, I have to get you to Carroll's on time as well."

"Carroll's?"

"Yes, sir. I believe their selection will best suit you. If Carroll's doesn't have what we want, there's always Armani, Gucci, Bataglia."

"Uh-uh. That's what *you* think. I'm up for one store, and that's it. What we don't find, you can go huntin' for. If they don't fit, they don't fit. I ain't lookin' to be Oscar de la Renta."

On the way to Carroll's, I gave Alan an earful.

"Gotta tell you, English, this is one event I'm just not up for."

"Should be a breeze for you, sir."

"Easy for you to say."

"Have you forgotten, sir, how many times I've driven you to black-tie affairs?" Knowing what he was thinking, I gave him a long look.

"Don't be a wiseass, English."

"Fact's fact, sir. Those were the days when your face graced the front page of every paper in town, suspected of murder, drug distribution, prostitution, fraud . . . what am I missing?"

"A few, you prick! How about the three-part article on my alleged connection with the top capos of the mob?"

"Oh, yes, I *did* forget that NBC story accusing you of being the government informant in the DeLorean case." Both of us laughed.

As I entered Carroll's, however, the laughter gave way to claustrophobia and then panic. My heart quickened, my mind raced, wanting to get the hell out. Dick Carroll, the store's proprietor, rushed toward us.

"Don't show your hand, sir," English whispered. "Be *the* Bob Evans!"

Dick stayed by my side as if he were my personal dresser, offering suggestion after suggestion. Desperate to get the fuck out, rather than model suit after suit, I accepted anything they put on. To everything, I said, "That's fine."

Fuck getting to the church on time. All I wanted was to get back to Woodland. That's where my head was.

What a difference a moment makes. A sudden surprise: Out of the adjoining dressing room appeared a wide smile and a genuine embrace. Art Buchwald.

"Bob! Great to see you!"

"You too, Art!"

"Bob, give it to me straight. Seersucker jackets? Don't they make me look squatty?"

"Ah, seersucker's for the young."

"Never liked seersucker anyway," Art chortled.

Forget politics—shopping in men's clothiers can sure breed strange bedfellows. We'd known each other for decades, but to my misfortune Art and I had never become close pals. Yet there we stood, smack in the middle of Carroll's, gossiping like two old yentas. Not about yesterday's bombshell—or scandalous infidelity—but rather of incidents forty years past. Our connective tissue: Mike Todd.

Mike was Art's closest friend as well as possibly the most important influence on my young life. His adventures—misadventures, gambling, hustling, and cocksmanship extraordinaire—were in a league of their own. Todd's infamous gambling exploits prompted Damon Runyon himself to tag him "the greatest natural gambler to ever cross my path."

He had such moxie that, even with empty pockets, he met and married the most royal movie star in the world: Elizabeth Taylor. So enraptured was Elizabeth at being Mrs. Todd that she not only changed her life, her name, and her religion (to Jewish, to please Mike, son of a rabbi), she even insisted that Todd be the chief executor of the Taylor family trust. Not bad for a guy who couldn't pay his own hotel bill.

Buchwald was among our country's best-regarded journalists. His recall of incidents and minutiae close to half a century past was spooky. How else could he remember Mike's fondness for me, including incidents even I had forgotten? Trying on another jacket, Buchwald laughed. "Mike told me you had more moxie than anyone—including himself. At sixteen, you were gambling for half a buck a point at gin . . . and winning, too. In those days, at a half a buck a point, you could lose fifteen to twenty grand in an afternoon."

"Never played for those stakes," I said. "Never won that big, but I was a winner—a big one! Many a Saturday I'd come home with my pockets full of green. And they weren't five-dollar bills."

"Mike gave me chapter and verse on you, Kid. That was his nickname for you." Buchwald laughed. "'A kid actor, playin' with the big boys, and takin' 'em pretty good. Now that's talent! Reminds me of me, only he's smarter. He enjoys the action. Me? I only enjoy playing when the stakes are higher than I can afford to lose. Big difference in age, yeah, but the Kid and me got off on the same action. Breakin' the rules. The guys who make 'em don't live by 'em, why the hell should we? Art, do you know why he's smarter than me? We both know that I made and blew a million bucks before I was twenty-one. Yeah, but Kid, he didn't lose it.'"

Art laughed again.

"Mike was an original. Never impressed by wealth. He had very few men friends—didn't have time. He had too many broads going for him. Broads were something else—gambling and broads were his turn-ons. But when your name came up, he was a different guy, Evans." He shook his head. "Told everybody that he'd bet his bankroll that you'd be a seven-figure guy by the time you hit thirty. Too bad everyone knew Mikey's pockets were change purses, so no one took him up on it."

Art broke off for a moment.

"Did you know, Kid, Mike's moxie spared no one, not even me. Do you wanna hear the best?"

Art proceeded to tell me the following story:

When *Around the World in Eighty Days* premiered in Washington, D.C., in late 1956, Art was a 50 percent partner and owner of the top Cantonese restaurant in town. Being a journalist certainly didn't leave him with deep pockets! It was constant pressure, making each week's payroll, food, booze, and accounts payable.

Back then, there were no credit cards. The bigger the politician, the quicker he signed the check! Try calling the Speaker of the House to get paid for an egg foo yong he signed for six months earlier. "In the best of times it was tough keeping up with your bills," Buchwald remembered.

Mike and Elizabeth were among Art's closest friends. Knowing it would be a big coup for his restaurant, they reserved it for the post-premiere bash of *Around the World in Eighty Days*.

Mike wanted the whole nine yards. He insisted that Art put up a huge tent adjacent to the restaurant and fill it with thousands of multicolored balloons. That way it would allow everyone attending the premiere the luxury of attending the post-bash as well!

Assiduously, Mike menued the evening for eleven hundred of his closest pals. Iranian Beluga caviar by the kilo. Cristal by the case. That ain't no cheap way out of town, pal!

When the kilos and the cases started disappearing with the speed of hot dogs at a football game, Art began to wonder how Mike was going to pay for it all. That mattered little to Mike, though. What did matter was that the who's who of Washington were out in full bloom, like never before. Why shouldn't they be?

Even in Washington, Beluga and Cristal are not the MO of evening gatherings. In Washington's inner circle, there was one rule: If you can't charge it, don't buy it!

The allure of the evening, however, wasn't the caviar or the champagne—or, for that matter, the film. Rather, it was their hostess, the most glamorous, sought-after, desired woman in the world, Elizabeth Taylor Todd.

It was after midnight. Buchwald was breathless, running back and forth between the tent and the restaurant. Like a nervous Jew, he kept checking to see if the president and first lady had arrived. Finally, paranoia overcame pragmatism, forcing Art to confront the party's host.

"Mike, the numbers are running high tonight. I'm just a journalist. Can't afford to vault these-size bills for long."

Mike interrupted, his face forlorn. "Do you think for a minute I'd leave you dry?" Feigning hurt, he looked at his watch. "It's one thirty now. The party should break up by three. Come by the Madison [the hotel where that night's 'royal couple' were staying] around noon tomorrow. We'll have some brunch and settle up then. Don't forget to bring the receipts," he said with a wink. "Need 'em for the record." He put his arms around Buchwald. "Hey, ain't it a great night? Come on! Let's get out of here and enjoy it. Hey, we deserve it!"

Mike's quick response to Art's problem would have put anyone else's mind to rest. Not Art. He knew Mike too fuckin' well. Minutes later, he cornered Elizabeth.

"See you tomorrow for brunch!"

"Wish we could darling, but we've got a plane on hold to fly us out at ten A.M. to Chicago. . . ."

Art let the moment pass. But not for long.

As the clock struck nine the next morning, Art struck home, ringing and ringing the fuckin' bell of the presidential suite till it opened. There stood Mike, already half dressed and packed to leave.

Buchwald was on fire. "Pay up, motherfucker!"

Without missing a beat, Mike threw his arm around Buchwald. "Just writing you a note. The bill's taken care of. Send it to Elizabeth's business manager. . . ."

"Where is Elizabeth? I want to confirm it with her."

"Sure." Mike smiled. "Elizabeth! Art's here. Wants to check something out with you."

Art proceeded to the royal bedroom . . . empty. Rushed back to the salon. Empty.

Naïvely, I interrupted Art, there in the dressing room at Carroll's.

"Do you think he meant to stiff you?"

Buchwald laughed so hard he had to take off his trifocals to handkerchief the tears running down his face.

"Stiff me? I'd still be on the corner waitin' . . . !"

18

Why is it that I was less secure walking into Sumner's party at Spago that Saturday night than I was a half century ago, walking onto Soundstage 16 at Universal Studios for my first screen gig, playing Irving Thalberg opposite the great Jimmy Cagney in *Man of a Thousand Faces*?

Afraid? Big-time! Wouldn't you be? My first scene in flicks and I'm telling Cagney how to act?

Lookin' back, it was a piece of cake compared to the cast I was about to face.

My date for the night was Paranoia, and she was diggin' her heels in but good. *You look like the straw man. No . . . the tin man. No . . .*

I hated to be rude to my date, but all I could think was . . .

Get the fuck out of my brain—and stay out!

• • •

The clock struck seven. My right foot was in the door and on the floor. Knowing Sumner as I did, I knew enough to make sure I was the first guest to arrive. Unfashionable? Sure, for anyone else. For Sumner, I would have showed up for dinner at eight in the morning.

I gave Wolfgang a hearty embrace, complimenting him on the evening's décor, and we walked over to the bar. Quickly, I ordered a triple straight scotch—with a straw. Didn't want to start the night by spilling a drink or letting it slip through my hand.

Surrounded by the evening's chosen, I was scared shitless.

The birthday boy quickly made his way toward me, wide-smiling.

"Was I right, pushing you to come?"

"Were you ever! First night out and I hit the jackpot! Wolfgang's outdone himself. I don't think he's ever done this for anyone else."

Within minutes, a steady flow of guests filled the room in their custom splendor. The flickering of hundreds of candles, the allure of the newest creations from dozens of couturiers: the evening had a magical aura. And yet, as the festivities shifted into high gear, I couldn't help thinking, *Something's wrong here.*

I'd known most of the guys there for years. To them, I'd always been looked upon as the Kid.

Now I caught myself in the mirror. *Have I aged that quickly?*

Perhaps I had. *But what the fuck am I complaining about?* I had a triple stroke. I was down for the count. And now I was back to talk about it.

All I needed was a hook. Something to carry me through the evening, head held high.

Serenaded by Stradivariuses, the guests glided to their antique French tables of eight, where Wolfgang's personally prepared foie gras awaited them.

Seventy-five years young, Sumner was like a kid, totally ingenuous, awed by the festivities in his honor. Though a billionaire many times over, at heart he was still a modest New England theater owner. My eye caught him standing alone in the back of the room, watching the celebration from afar.

His expression said it all: *Is this really happening to me?*

Sneaking up, I kissed him on the cheek. "You're gonna outlive all of us, you motherfucker!"

He smiled.

"Give it to ya straight, Sumner. You're the only guy in town who could have pulled this cast together. I ain't easy to please, and you know it! But tonight breaks the mold."

He blushed like a kid hearing his first *I love you.*

And, just like that, the expression on his face gave me my hook: Grant 'em.

That's right: *Cary Grant* 'em.

Learned from the best. Mr. Cleft Chin himself. From the time we met, until the last time he closed his eyes, we were never more than seven digits away from one another. He's the only guy I've ever met who had more panache walking into a room backward than anyone walking into a room forward. A master of self-deprecation: Throughout the years, he enjoyed telling people, "I'm really not that good an actor. I just know how to play myself better than anyone else."

To me, he said it with a wink: "Be yourself. It's easier."

I saw Cary's charm in action when I was his personal guest at the premiere of *An Affair to Remember*. It was one memorable night—not so much for the film, but rather for what followed. The reviews had come in, and they were underwhelming. But Cary knew not to show and tell—a knack that made Archie Leach, the real man, as dangerous a poker player as Cary Grant, the actor. Whoever approached him that night, I watched as he preempted their false congratulations by deflecting his attention right back onto them—complimenting their name, their family, their health, their business. And then he was on to another. So masterful his charm, not one had an inkling what hit them.

I'm gonna Grant 'em, I thought.

Gonna Cary Grant the ones who ask me about my stroke.

I made my way to our table but made sure I was the last to sit down. Checking the table's cast, I knew one thing: This was gonna be one tough gig. I knew all seven of my dinner partners. All top pros, all looking to play *Information, Please!* It was crisis time.

A tub of caviar surrounded by crème fraîche, slices of lime, and potato shells . . . it was a table set to feast. If I tried to pick up a knife, fork, or spoon, though, I knew it could blow my cover before I said a fuckin' word.

Instead, I resolved to shock them.

I wide-smiled the inquisitive round table.

"Wolfgang's somethin' else! He's transformed Spago to Maxim's at its best."

A theatrical pause, then a quick look to Sherry Lansing. "My luck! Nothing's a bigger turn-on to me than caviar and potato shells and I can't touch it. It's the one day of the year I can't even have a drink! Tomorrow, of all days, I've got an unbreakable appointment at Cedars."

"Darling, change it," Sherry purred. "Who's your doctor?"

"Kivowitz!"

"Oh, he'll change it. Easily."

"Don't think so, Sherry. Set in stone. Of all the machinery at Cedars, they've lined up their prized computer rig to evaluate me. They're the only place in the country that has it. That thing's got a longer waiting list than any of our pictures."

She laughed. "We're in the wrong business, then."

"You said it, I didn't. I called Kivowitz this morning in Aspen, trying to tell him tomorrow's impossible for me. He says he's personally flying in—*be there at seven, no later*—and he hangs up. I couldn't tell him my extenuating circumstances were a night out at Spago's."

Birthday Host Redstone walked over to the table. "Hope everyone's enjoying themselves."

Candy Spelling took his hand. "Sumner, you certainly know how to bring out the best in people. Never seen Spago light up like tonight."

Suddenly his eye caught my empty plate. In a commanding officer's tone: "Start eating or I'll think you don't like the food."

"Don't worry about me, Sumner, I'm just a slow starter."

Luckily, he was called away to another table.

"He's my boss, but he checks in on me like I'm the night watchman," I said to Daryl Hannah, sitting next to me. "If he comes back, can we switch plates?"

Twenty minutes later, the birthday boy was on his way back.

Quick on the pickup, Daryl cut her soufflé in half and switched plates. When the birthday boy got there, I blurted out: "Wow! I wish I could package Wolfgang's cooking, Sumner. Could be a good Viacom subsidiary."

He came. He saw. He laughed. He left.

Thank God. I got away with it. Kissing Daryl's cheek, "Thanks for them reflexes."

Close to an hour now, and still not a sign that anyone suspected that I was anything but in top form. All I had to do was make my way through dessert. *Well, I'm finally into my third act*, I thought.

"Aaron," I asked Spelling, "do you think the birthday boy's gonna make another round?"

"I'll go over and talk with him, and keep him where he is for a while."

"Mr. Spelling? I owe you big for that one!"

"You're right—you do."

Jackie Bisset started to laugh. "Bob, this reminds me of going to a Royal Post Premiere dinner in London. I was seated at the royal table and—just like clockwork—as soon as we sat down, I became royally nauseous. Too afraid to eat a thing . . . but too scared to be disrespectful. Without even thinking to excuse myself to the loo, somehow I made it through the entire dinner. Charm got me through the meal without anyone noticing I hadn't touched a morsel. Isn't it bizarre, Bob, that watching is so much more painful than doing?"

Thank you, Jackie, I said to myself. *You just jump-started my third act.*

I got the table's attention. "Got to give you a great story about watching."

"I'm sure you can give us a lot of stories about watching, Bob," cracked Arnold Kopelson.

"I could, Arnold, but it'd be too boring for you. Do any of you remember Jean Negulesco, the director?"

Dominick Dunne: "Do I remember? I worked with him at Fox. Directed some of the best romances. *Three Coins in the Fountain* . . ."

"He also did *The Best of Everything*, a picture I was in."

"Not one of his best," Dunne quipped back.

"It was for me. Playing in that picture for me, with one of the female leads . . ."

"Which one?" asked Candy.

"Kiss-and-don't-tell has been my style since before you were born, Candy. Let's just say, a guard saw the both of us leave my Winnebago at two in the morning, and within forty-eight hours the whole lot knew about it.

"When he found out, Negulesco walked into my dressing room. Didn't say a word. Then, in his European style, he shrugged. 'Robert, one day you are going to be like me.' I didn't know what the fuck he was talking about.

"'When I was your age, all I wanted to do was make love to every leading lady I worked with. As I got older, I used to like to *watch* people make love. Today, now, I like to watch the people who *watch* the people who make love.

"'Enjoy it while you can, Bob. Everyone's the same. The older you get, the more watching becomes better than the doing.'

"That's what he said, Jackie. But he was wrong! Whether it be food, sex—anything—the doing is still more fun than the watching."

By the time I finished, the dessert had arrived. I'd made it to the finish line. Couldn't believe I'd pulled it off.

What had started out a potential horror show ended up as one of the most memorable nights in years.

Wherever you are, Archie, I thought, *I hope I did you proud. Were you ever right! Not one of them even asked about my stroke!*

19

Two days before Turkey Day, 1998. As the clock struck noon, I hit Spago, the top luncheon rendezvous in Beverly Hills. My luncheon date was no beauty—rather, my beady-eyed locust attorney. The subject? My will.

It would be a quick lunch and a quick will. Doesn't take long to divide nothing.

When I got there, I looked around and realized I was the only guy in the joint. Grabbing the bar phone, I quick-dialed my secretary. "Where the hell is the locust? He's five minutes late already."

"Mr. Evans, I'm terribly sorry. I tried to reach you. I've made a mistake. The lunch was actually set for one, not twelve."

"Sorry's no answer! If you can't get a luncheon date straight, how the hell can I depend on you to even open the mail?"

"Mr. Evans, you must get a cell phone, like everyone else."

"Oh, really? Get this straight—I'm not a doctor. I'm not a hooker. And I don't like . . . being . . . on . . . call. End of subject."

I banged down the phone. My eyes spanned the elegant Spago, still being dressed for lunch. There was Wolfgang himself, checking the tables, reservations, flowers, and every nuance that makes Spago singular. Wolfgang spotted me at the bar and came over.

"Bob, did you hear? They're doing a book on me! *The Kid Stays in the Kitchen!*"

Both of us laughed. A fond embrace between two old friends of many decades.

"What are you doing here this early?"

"Thought we'd talk turkey, and you ain't easy to catch."

"Come! We have a drink in the back together." He led me over to a booth.

"Don't get it, Wolf. It's been thirty years, and you're faster on your feet now than you were then. There ain't no better sprint runner. Kitchen to the table, table to the kitchen. How do you do it?"

"I love it, that's how."

"You're a lucky kraut. The wealthiest I know. How few people love what they do." Our drinks arrived. I raised my glass. "The past we can't do anything about, the future is unknown. A Thanksgiving Day toast to the present!"

"Ah, but the past was such fun!"

I couldn't help but wide-smile. It sure as hell was.

"You were a kid chef at Ma Maison, right? And your boss, what was his name . . . ? Patrick Terrail!"

"Patrick Terrail was not a restaurant man, Bob. He was the

son of the top restaurateur in all of France—Claude Terrail. And competitive, too. He wanted desperately to be a success, and that's where the hitch came. He knew I was the key to that success. So even in my twenties I had, as you would say, the run of the house. No one knew the kitchen better than me, because I loved it! I could make any dish better. And when you have the key, you can open many a door. Money? I couldn't have cared less. But I had one thing no other chef had—my own private table in the restaurant. It was front and center, and it was mine alone to seat."

"Why was that important?"

"I looked at it every day as my party. Money could not buy you entrance. It was Wolfgang's corner. *That,* to me, was wealth. Patrick didn't like it at all. But he had no choice. It was either Wolf or the wolves would be after him. Without Wolf, Ma Maison would have been a hamburger joint in a month."

"You couldn't have been that good at that age!"

"I was. I worked sixteen hours a day, eight in the kitchen and eight at Puck's round table of eight. You know what's crazy, Bob? No money could buy a seat at Wolfgang's table. It was full-time reserved." A reflective laugh. "There I was, just a chef . . . and every day I hosted Woody Allen, Helmut Newton, Jackie Bisset, Farrah Fawcett, Gianni Agnelli, Richard Burton, Jack Nicholson, Warren Beatty, Alain Delon, and of course you! Then, I was a snob. Today, I'm just rich. You have no idea how I had to switch tables and reservations when you and Delon would come. Why do you think I never charged you? Ach, there's not a table in the city that touches it today."

"Never will be, Wolf."

"I learned something as a chef when I was very young. Inverse snobbism—it's the only dish the wealthiest can't afford to order."

"Wolf, man or woman, who was the hottest ticket ever to sit at your table?"

"A man? I'm sorry to say this to you, Bob, but by far it was Alain Delon. When rumors went around that he'd be there, reservations would go up twenty percent. All women!"

"How about women? C'mon, concentrate. I'll bet you come up with a name."

Wolf sat for a moment, concentrating. Then, taking a pen from his pocket, he slowly wrote a name and quickly covered it with a napkin. "Let's see how good my memory is. Pick up the napkin, Bob."

I did . . . then stared him straight in the eye. "You fuckin' kraut! You hit the bull's-eye."

"How could I forget her, Bob? It was she who made me a celebrity. . . ." He laughed gently. "But I was scared shitless having Madame Claude herself use Ma Maison as her hangout. What a dummkopf! Thought she would close the restaurant in a week."

He leaned closer and half whispered, "If Patrick had known who she was, he'd never have let her in. But without Madame Claude, Ma Maison would never have become Ma Maison. Remember those Saturdays? It was Madame Claude, Pierre Galleut, Alain Delon, and you. Claude once told me that between San Diego and San Francisco, she had at least thirty clients, all very wealthy, who married her girls. There wasn't a girl who wouldn't be happy to hear from her. But she would never call or ask for anything."

"A fuckin' madam with a princely pride. And now she was

living in L.A., trying to start a pastry business. Ripley wouldn't believe it. 'Los Angeles is not for me,' she used to say. 'But you know, Robert, I can't go back to France.' And she was right. As soon as she got off the plane, she would have been arrested and put in jail for murder."

"Murder?" Wolfgang's face was ashen.

"M-U-R-D-E-R. That's right. She was set up by the government. Knew too much, but they couldn't kill her. I was having lunch one day with Alain when Claude joined us. God, was she an unhappy madam. 'Alain, I'll never be able to go back to France. Here I am in Los Angeles, selling pastry. I hate eating pastry, never mind selling it. I like pussy and I like selling pussy. If only I could change my name . . . but I can't do that, either.'

"The sad thing is, without Claude, Paris just ain't Paris. Forget all the sex—there were more clandestine meetings in her little office than they have at the State Department. She was the hub of the action. It's amazing how sex brings business to the table. And she sure knows the table. What a waste of talent . . . seeing her sell doughnuts in L.A."

We reflected on the bumpy roads of fate. "You and Alain were always in here together."

"How about for over a decade we were joined at the hip?"

"That long?" He shook his head. "And you're still here to talk about it?"

"Let's just say it wouldn't have made a Disney flick."

We got up and I put my arm around him.

"When you see him, please thank Alain for making Ma Maison the place to be."

"I don't have to tell him, Wolf. He knows it."

20

From the early sixties to the mid-eighties, Alain Delon was the highest-paid actor in the history of France. For more than twenty years, Delon dominated France's international box office. Having starred in fifty-nine films, making his debut in 1958, he was a god in every country in the world except one . . . the United States. *Purple Noon, Rocco and his Brothers, Eclipse, The Leopard, Le Samourai, Borsalino*—one classic followed another, vaulting him into the role of the world's top romantic leading male actor . . . almost.

Reflect and you'll realize, shocking as it may be, how few European leading men have became stars in America—at least among those for whom English isn't their native tongue. That goes for women as well—with the exception of Ingrid Bergman. (Sophia Loren started as a film star, but as an actress she made a great armpiece for a male star.) There's a reason for this: between New York and Los Angeles there is a huge valley called the United States of America. And since the advent of talking pictures, the populace of that huge valley does not pay highly to hear accents.

Delon was the man to break the mold—or so the studios thought. Delon himself couldn't have cared less. Hey, it's tough living more luxuriously than a king. Half Corsican, half French, he was one tough, smart motherfucker. I mean *tough* in the physical way, and smart in every way. From art to francs, he mastered them all. At the age of seventeen he arrived in Paris, where he worked as an usher in a cinema. He told people, "In one year, my name will be on the marquee."

Well, the impossible happened. Within a year, he was on not one marquee, but three. In forty years, his name never came off.

In 1961, I got my cinematic romantic break in Twentieth Century Fox's flick of the year, *The Best of Everything*, playing King Prick. The picture was hailed by the press, but I sure in hell was no Delon. My publicity far overshadowed my performance . . . and at that time publicity mattered far more than performance. I was press-hot, and Fox cared more about pressing the press than coddling the critics. Off to Europe I went. I was getting more fan mail at the time than anyone at Twentieth, with the exception of Elvis Presley. He could sing and dance. Me? I just had a profile and a reputation . . . not good, but prone to ink wherever I traveled.

It was a once-in-a-lifetime high and I wanted to suck it all up. And suck it up I did!

Knowing my penchant for gambling, a friend of mine, Dr. Paul Albou, asked me to join him in a high-stakes poker game. It lasted till six in the morning. There were two people left in the game, Evans . . . and Alain Delon.

That's how we met.

The weeks, months, and years we spent together were exciting, dangerous, cavalier, debaucherous, decadent, and electrifying. If I tried to capture everything that happened in those years in those books, the critics would think I was on an acid trip. The only thing more shocking than those twenty years is that I'm here, alive, to write about it.

For close to two decades, Delon and I were great pals and confidants to each other's most private affairs. Our bond of trust was sacrosanct. The adventures we shared, the rules we broke, the secrets we kept, could be told only in the confessional booth. Together we were like two confidence guys, getting that vicarious thrill that can only be gotten by pressing the danger button. Did it work? On all fronts!

Neither of us was unscathed by our skydiving actions. He, a celebrated film star not only in France but, with the exception of America, throughout the world, was temporarily barred from France for his alleged tangential involvement in a murder. (He was eventually cleared of all charges.) Me, the boy wonder of Paramount, almost ended up in the slammer for cocaine, murder, fraud, and prostitution. That's for openers.

From 1963 to 1965 we were both married. Alain married Nathalie Barthélémy, and I got hitched to Camilla Sparv, the sensational Swede. For two years they lived in Los Angeles while he was starring in Universal's *Texas Across the River.* Camilla and I occupied a small house in Bel Air. I went from being a half-assed actor into becoming a virgin producer at Twentieth Century Fox. As married couples, all four of us enjoyed gambling. Three or four nights a week we played gin. The stakes were high: One night Camilla and I won close to fifty thousand dollars.

By the end of two years, Alain and I were on the single path again. He moved back to Paris and started making film after film, and I express-trained it to becoming head honcho of Paramount Pictures. It was a chaotic time for us both.

In 1966, I found myself in Paris. I hadn't seen Alain for some time, but when he picked me up at the Plaza Athénée it was as if we'd just seen one another a day before. Ours being friendship treasured, our time apart meant little.

Alain was so proud to see me, a fellow actor, become head of a major studio that he gave the most elegant party one could give—at the fabled Maxim's. The next day he picked me up for lunch at the Relais-Plaza, *the* restaurant in Paris. Money could not buy you entrance. Here we were, the biggest romantic movie star in the world, and me, his pal, Hollywood's bachelor du jour. Delon always had a table reserved and if he didn't show, no one could use it.

The maître d' met us at the door and escorted us to Delon's table. Passing the bar, I noticed Jorge Guinle, one of the wealthiest men in Brazil. His family owned the Copacabana Palace Hotel as well as the entire beachfront of Rio. An attractive man, he had only one deficit in life: his height. In stocking feet he touched a bit over five feet tall. He was, in my lingo, a sitting personality—

the same height standing as sitting. (Too many times I've eyed some beauty across a crowded room, and approached the table with my mouth agape . . . only to discover she was a sitting personality. Hello and good-bye in sixty seconds.)

Cuddling beside Jorge was a stunning beauty. But she was no sitting personality, she was the real thing, a knockout nearly six feet tall. What a difference a foot makes. Naturally, I greeted him with more friendliness than ever.

"Hi, Jorge. How good to see you!" But I wasn't looking at him—rather, above him, at the most striking brunette I'd seen in all of France. Her green eyes matched his bulging pockets. Her smile reminded me of Ava Gardner.

In our brief conversation, she mentioned that she'd just graduated from the University of Berlin and was in Paris for the first time. I bid them a quick good-bye and sat down with Alain at his table.

Begrudgingly, I asked him the $64,000 question. "I can't eat, Alain. I'm sick. I just don't understand it. Look at us. Not a bad parlay to know eights, nines, or tens. What I don't understand is that, between us, we don't have two girls who equal a ten . . . and here's this midget, sitting at the bar with a full ten! What's worse, she seems to be in love with him!"

Casting his eyes over toward their table, he gave the beauty his Delon look; she noticed but paid no attention. He turned back to me. "Within forty-eight hours she'll be in my bed."

Now that's chutzpah, French style.

"Bob, let's get out of here. Take a walk." Walk we did, down the Champs-Élysées, toward the Arc de Triomphe. Mind you, not one head failed to turn to see if that was really the macho hero in the flesh. Delon being Delon, he never changed his expression, never turned his head, even when he spoke.

"Left at the corner."

"Where are we going?"

"Number thirteen, rue du Carre."

"What's there?"

"An elevator."

I knew him all too well: Whether it was the press, an associate, a friend, or a lady fair, silence was his answer to curiosity. *Well, I'm on his turf*, I thought. *Might as well play by his rules.*

Across the street from the *Herald Tribune* building, we arrived at a narrow office building about eight stories high. We walked through a revolving door toward a rickety, tiny gated French elevator. Reaching the top floor, we walked to the end of the hall and opened the door. Behind the desk sat a rather average-looking lady, who jumped up at the sight of Alain, put her arms around him, and kissed him. Then again, who wouldn't?

"Claude, I'd like you to meet my closest friend, Bob Evans. He is my host whenever I am in America. When I stay in his home, I'm treated as royalty. Now he is visiting me in my home. The only way I can show my appreciation is to treat him the same."

She extended her hand. "Monsieur, Paris is yours."

With the deliberate authority of a network news anchor, Alain continued: "Claude travels the world several times a year. Be it Scotland, Ethiopia, Brazil, Denmark, Spain, Morocco, Argentina, she has but one purpose: She seeks out one who has the most panache, charm, beauty, and all the attributes, to be groomed to perfection."

Stupidly, I blurted, "Are you the French associate for Eileen Ford or Elite?"

Cutting me off disdainfully, Claude responded. "Non, monsieur. I am not a modeling agent." A rare laugh from Delon.

"Robert, Claude has no partner. She has a mini-monopoly."

"Monopoly of what?"

"Of the world's most valuable asset."

I wasn't too quick on the uptake.

"She seeks out women of the world who have the potential of perfection, and if they meet her criteria, and after spending time with them and coming to a mutual understanding, she makes an investment, turning near perfection into the real thing. One thing about Claude, Robert: She puts her money where her mouth is. Each girl she selects is groomed from head to toe, from clothes to cosmetics to manners. It's a big investment, but the payday by far exceeds the outlay. Many times she has spent one hundred thousand dollars molding—"

"Alain, many times more!"

Alain looked at me. "You see? That's why Claude is a monopoly." I was both chilled and thrilled at the same time.

"Close your eyes, Robert, and think. The best-looking girls from throughout the entire world are at Claude's disposal. All of them are there, waiting for your call. Many a young beauty flies to Paris hopeful of meeting Claude. Some wait weeks, some wait months. The few who are selected are put under Claude's umbrella, to be groomed to be royal paramours. Many of them have ended up as royalty—figuratively or literally."

Claude confirmed his account. "Alain, no one knows better than yourself. To be a Claude girl, you must be totally submissive to the desires of my client's wishes, no matter what the wishes are. One mistake, and they are no longer with Madame Claude. It doesn't happen often."

Alain smiled. "I want you to know, Robert, you've just met the most powerful and influential woman in all of France."

Me? I'm thinking to myself, Fuck Italy. France is the place to make films!

I looked at Claude. "Don't mean to be nosy, but . . . is that a bed in the next room?"

Claude answered my stupid question. "Yes, Monsieur. It's there for . . . call it a patriotic reason. Many a powerful man from the government needs an afternoon siesta. Their schedules are so pressured. All it takes is a call to Claude, the time they wish to have their rest, and a description of the companion or companions they wish to rest with. Naturally, there is a separate entrance to the room; this door is usually closed."

"Hmmm. Interesting."

A wide smile from Delon. "At last! I have a chance to pay you back for your hospitality. You would think a movie star would be spoiled, but you really spoiled me every time I was at your home." He laughed. "But you're more spoiled than me. How can I pay you back for all the pleasures you've given me? I offer you Claude, on a silver platter . . . to please whatever your palate may desire."

"You must understand, Monsieur Evans, as long as Claude is alive, never shall a Claude girl accept a gratuity from you. If I find out she does, at the end of the day she will not be a Claude girl."

I turned to Delon. "Alain, this goes down as the most extraordinary gift I've ever received. There ain't nothin', and I mean nothin', that runs a distant second. You sure bull's-eyed it, you prick."

I felt like I'd won the lottery. Alain and I embraced and laughed and laughed. . . .

Claude escorted us back to the elevator. When the rickety gate opened, four legs began to tremble. It couldn't be. Was this a trick? The very girl I'd fallen in love with earlier that day was staring right at me!

Without a word, we descended to Delon's car. We went back to the Plaza Athénée. The breathtaker? She was one of Claude's fillies. She could've been the next Mrs. Evans. (I guess I wasn't the only one who felt that way. She went on to become the wife of the second-richest man in Germany, heir to one of the great industrial fortunes.)

And Claude? In the late 1970s she was forced to flee France, victim of her own notoriety. Seems all them politicians and powerful men let their fear of exposure get the better of them. She was the subject of three movies, many books, and endless investigations before she returned to France in 1986—to arrest, trial, and jail.

If it be true that the world's oldest profession competes with any of the world's oldest commodities—gold, silver, diamonds—then Madame Claude could go toe-to-toe with the world's most entrepreneurial financial geniuses.

Three days after things ended with Catherine, a three-page spread appeared in *People* magazine: "The Nuptial Bliss of the Princess and the Player." There was a slight problem. Unbeknownst to all, the Princess had already dumped the Player.

As it was Catherine's first trip to the altar, gifts from all over the world were arriving at our home. Calls of congratulations were keeping all six lines busy. There was one problem: Catherine wasn't there to receive them. She was at her lawyer's office working on her annulment.

It was Dodge City time. I couldn't take the heat. I had to get the hell out of there, and quick. An hour later, I was limping down the beaches of Laguna, after checking into a nearby hotel under the alias Tony Lombardo. I was a mental and physical cripple, trying to escape a very public embarrassment.

All I could think was, *This has happened to me before.* It was forty years ago—exactly forty, in the summer of '58. What a long forty years. But suddenly it felt like it was happening all over again.

I was still a young movie star. Romantically linked with cinema's top femme fatales—Ava Gardner, Lana Turner, Grace Kelly—I was nicknamed "Lover Boy" by the Hollywood press.

Then it happened. I met the girl of my dreams, Danielle Loder, and she hit me where it hurt.

Extraordinarily beautiful. Stylish to the tens. Deep-freeze cool. Hey, what do you expect? She's a fuckin' Frenchie. They breed 'em that way!

Her father, John Loder, a famous English matinee idol; her mother, Micheline Cheirel, a renowned French actress. Strangely, Danielle had zero interest in being an actress. That alone made her one big turn-on. Without trying, she stood tall as one of the world's top models. From head to toe, she was it! My every fantasy, finally a reality. *The future Mrs. Evans*, I thought.

Did I flip for her? Big-time! Did she for me? Who the fuck knows? Did I have all the props? *Big-time!* A lot of good it did me!

Danielle was on my arm as we walked down the red carpet at the Paramount Theatre in New York at the premiere of *The Best of Everything*, Twentieth Century Fox's big flick of the year. Me? I starred as "Lover Boy." Not a bad setup for a guy trying to seduce a dame. Them mobs of girls, busting through them ropes, grabbin' and screamin' for my autograph . . .

Did it impress Danielle? Less than zero! Her only emotion

was boredom—boredom with the film, with the night . . . with me!

Did I pick up Frenchie's vibes? Of course not—I'm a guy!

A month later, rolling over on one of the silky beaches in the Bahamas, I asked her to marry me.

"Why not?" she whispered back.

Don't let anyone tell you different. Them fuckin' Frenchies have fuckin' down to a science!

Me? I couldn't take the heat—not from Danielle, from the thermometer. It never went south of 101. Too hot for me! We left two days early. She, to Paris and Milan for the Couturier Collections. Me, I flew in the other direction, having had the luck to cop the second male lead to Yves Montand in Jerry Wald's production of *Let's Make Love,* starring Marilyn Monroe. Playing King Prick in *The Best of Everything* had jumpstarted my career back into high gear. Not only did that film set me up for *Let's Make Love*; it awakened Darryl Zanuck to the fact that I was still his protégé, the only actor he had under personal contract.

Living in Paris, Zanuck got wind of his protégé's nuptial news. Why not announce his engagement to the world? Take over Maxim's, make it the party of the year? "Lover Boy and Loder getting hitched!" Not a bad headline for a night to remember.

The party was scheduled for a Saturday night. I planned to arrive in Paris the previous Tuesday, to meet Danielle's family, see Paris for the first time—then top it off with Zanuck's engagement blast. Well, that's not quite the way it worked out.

First of all, Marilyn kept the production waiting on script changes. Days turned into a week, a week into two . . . and still

no Monroe. Time was ticking away! It was either save my engagement or wait for the Diva Monroe. I opted for the former, leaving
Monroe a note: "I knew you when, Kid!"

Monroe didn't take kindly to my sarcasm. Within twenty-four
hours, I was replaced.

Instead of arriving on Tuesday, I landed in Paris four hours
before the bash. The publicity honchos from Twentieth were
there en masse. Yeah, but front and center stood the love of my
life, looking more beautiful than ever. Not a bad way to step off
a plane on your first trip to Paris!

Then, in the backseat of the limo on our way to the Plaza
Athénée for a quick change, Danielle cooed, "I'm so in love."

Throwing my arms around her. "Me too, darling."

"I met a Greek. His name is Fivos. I'm madly in love with
him." Paris? Suddenly it looked like Pittsburgh.

"Danielle, in three hours, Zanuck's announcing our engagement to the world."

"I know."

"People from all over Europe are flying in for the night."

"I know."

"You couldn't tell me on the phone?"

"I felt that wasn't fair. I wanted to look at you—tell you eye
to eye."

"Not fair! Danielle—that's a thirteen-thousand-mile look!"

"I know!"

"I blew off Marilyn Monroe for you!"

"I know!"

"Zanuck's my boss. He's the one throwing this engagement
party!"

With the coolness of a blackjack dealer, she interrupted me. "Well . . . we'll play it out."

Play it out we did. An Academy Award nightmare. Them flashbulbs . . . them paparazzi . . . them congratulations. My first trip to Paris, my first engagement—both of them disasters!

At two in the morning, she dropped me off at the Plaza Athénée. Ah! But with a kiss—not to build a dream on, nor to give me a hard-on, but to say good night and good-bye, forever!

I couldn't sleep. And I didn't stay for breakfast. I snuck out the service entrance, hailed a cab, and hopped the first plane back to the States.

Over the Atlantic I got up to use the john. Not to take a piss, but to take a long look at myself in the mirror. First time out, I'm dumped at the altar. Depressed? Yeah—but for the wrong reasons. Not over love lost, but over ego crushed.

What am I supposed to tell people? I blew off Monroe for some Frenchie who was sleeping with a Greek? Uh-uh, don't tell no one. Those motherfuckers would enjoy it too much. Truth's truth: The only thing that gets the gossipers jealous is heat. When you hang your hat in the frying pan, it brings out their envy, and when you catch fire, that envy turns to hate. Some town, Hollywood, huh?

Good-bye, Paris, Hello Frying Pan. Feeling stratospheric, I walked out of the john with my ego on high, tapping the shoulder of a striking-looking stewardess.

"How about a double Bloody?"

"A twist of lemon?"

"If *you* twist it."

A wicked smile, "I'll twist it good."

Reclining in my plush seat, she approached with cocktail in hand. "Hope you like the twist. It's my specialty."

I wide-smiled, thinking to myself, *Evans, you're back in action.*

From my teens to my sixties, three pastimes remained my secret treasures of life. Irony is, the three shared the same first letter: sun . . . sports . . . and sex.

Be it surfing, swimming, sailing, skiing, or just plain lyin' on a beach, feeling the hot rays of the blessed sun by day, allowed thoughts to emerge from my head—ones that would never have come into play in the merry-go-round called civilization.

And I never appreciated it. I took them all for granted, never giving a pregnant thought to how blessed I was by the Guy Upstairs.

Though the two be diametric to each other, sports and sex crossed the finish line in a dead heat. After I became head honcho at Paramount in 1966, my ultimate fantasy became a reality: buying a home I could call my own. Was I indecisive as to what my fantasy could be? Quite the contrary. With maniacal specificity, I warned all brokers not to bother me unless they could genuinely fulfill my exact needs. Not having the patience nor the time to be a looker, I let it be known clearly that I had two prerequisites:

1. **That the home not be ostentatious.**
2. **That the property have enough land to build the best fuckin' tennis court in the land.**

It took more than a year of searching . . . but falling in love ain't easy. When it was done, I'd found my life's partner.

Did I design and construct the best tennis court in all of California? You bet your ass I did!

Many a man's fantasy is a luxury yacht, or private plane. Why, I don't know. I've never been a great tennis player, but having the finest tennis court in town was my ultimate turn-on. Though my name was low on the list of the talent who graced the court, I spent many of the greatest times of my life playing on it.

Gene Mako, the world's premier designer of professional tennis courts, maestroed a court that to this day has not been matched. Its special lighting makes night tennis more visible than day. The furor it caused made the City Council of Beverly Hills ban the installation of stadium lights forever.

No matter who the celebrity, they came to Woodland to play day tennis at night. More action took place on that court—from Jimmy Connors, John McEnroe, and Bobby Riggs, to every major player, hustler, and movie star—than any other. Magazines wrote more about my court than my films. It got to a point where

I needed a special secretary just to book the court for the greatest players in the world, who all wanted to play at Woodland when they passed through Los Angeles.

Legitimate or otherwise, many's the clandestine encounter closed, sealed, and delivered on Woodland's tennis court. Money could not buy you entrance: Only the closest were invited. As the years passed, it became the most restricted club in all of Los Angeles. Its celebrity remains mythical even today. If it were anyone else's court, I would never have been allowed entrance. Wouldn't have blamed them, either.

But it was my jewel, and mine to choose.

Between swimming, tennis, and a variety of other sports, I never stopped feeling like a teenager. And that's wealth that money can't buy, pal!

Now let's get it on, to the biggest *S . . . sex.*

At its best, the allure of the chase is like being strapped in the front seat of the most frightening, dangerous roller coaster ever built. Both highs are close to hallucinogenic. The difference is, at the end of the roller-coaster ride, you get off and turn your attention to the other joys of the amusement park. Not so at the end of the biblical high. When you're done with that, the thrill is gone. The pain stays . . . and stays . . . and stays, never seeming to heal. Like barnacles, they just keep holdin' . . . givin' you them headaches, them heartaches . . .

In consolation, everything in life is temporary, including life itself. Fuck it! Never allow an attack of the heart to give you a heart attack. It ain't worth it!

From the time I was a teenager enjoying my first sexual pleasures, I got drunk on the power that came with it. A connection was forged, almost electrical in its immediacy. I was consumed by this newfound world, adventurous, obsessed. Was I a pioneer in these uncharted waters? You bet your ass! At least I thought I was. It was a pleasure I couldn't deny myself, or *wouldn't* deny myself. It was by far my greatest joy.

Thrilling, exhilarating, scandalous, and yes, destructive.

Upon reflection, did its power serve me harshly or kindly? It's difficult to answer, as every year I have a different take on its influence on my life's bumpy road.

From my late teens through my twenties, my sexual liaisons kept me constantly on the radar of the gossip locusts, whose exaggerations earn them their weekly paycheck. After a while it doesn't matter. There's nothin' you can do about it. Once branded, always branded. Infamy became my calling card.

Even after royalty fades, infamy stays. Truth be told, what's more boring than royalty? And what's more enticing than the down-and-dirties of infamy?

Fuck it! Take a bit of fatherly advice, from one who's still branded with the baggage of infamy: ENJOY IT! ACCEPT IT. EMBRACE IT!

Infamy can be the most seductive prop in your bag of tricks.

Let's pay a little closer attention to those big three *S*'s. Considering the fact that I was not rigorously practicing for the Olympics, but, rather, stressed to the tens—reporting to junior G-men who knew nothing about the cinema beyond the price of a ticket—

my libido was travelin' north at a surprising rate, while it should have been going south.

Here's a secret: For a full decade before the fat lady sang, my doctors had been telling me I was a perfect candidate for a stroke. Immortal am I, my ego shouted from within. Being sixty-seven bothered me little. I felt like a kid.

Trouble was, I acted like one, too.

That black bag was unzipped and waiting for me. I must have stepped over it, rather than in it. Never could find anything without my glasses. But you can't beat the odds on everything.

Let's take my pleasures three:

I had three strokes, flatlined, saw the white light, and within months there I was, hitting a backhand on the tennis court. Sounds like a fairy tale, huh?

Well, dying and coming back to life isn't quite as romantic as it may sound. Every morning I had to ingest a minimum of eight pills, changing every week or so in a constant carousel of new and torturous medications. The potential cures often seemed to carry as much pain and bodily insult as the disease. At times, all that pharmacology made me feel as if I were imprisoned in some camp and being experimented on.

After the fat lady sang, all my bodily pleasures took a backseat. The hot rays of the sun were now off-limits, as were the hot breasts of a sunny girl. The reason was simple: Every pill I swallowed, without exception, had some dangerous effect. They thinned my blood, blocked calcium deposits throughout my body, pressured my blood pressure down from the 200s to the low 100s, and relaxed my muscles—and that was before the army of antidepressants. Between morning, noon, and evening, I ingested more than twenty pills a day.

There's no fuckin' doctor on earth that can give you a read-out of how one of these twenty pills interacts with the nineteen others. But I can unequivocally attest to the one thing they did accomplish. The warning statement on each pill packet, without exception, advises the patient—in very small type—that the medication is likely to dampen sexual desire, potency, and/or sexual performance. Many even go as far as stating that they may nullify your sexual desires.

Meanwhile, blood thinners carry a label that warns of great danger if the patient should be exposed to sunlight.

Wait a minute, I asked my doctor. I can't play tennis. I can't sit in the sun, or even in the water when it's sunny out. And I can't fuck. Is that true, Doc?

With one look, he put my situation back in perspective. "You're alive, aren't you?"

That said it all.

Reality does bite back. Many a time, them pills made my heart all but go through my chest. I felt like my head was goin' to blow off.

Whenever I stood up from a sitting position and failed to count to ten before I moved, I'd have to grab on to the nearest chair, or risk collapsing onto the ground. Forget tennis, forget the sun, forget sex—when you get up in the middle of the night to take a piss, get dizzy, then slowly bend to the floor and crawl back to bed without making it to the john, you know it's time to change gears or get out of town.

"Doctor, I'm takin' twenty-one pills a day. My head's about to explode. I ain't gonna be a toilet for any more of these pharmaceutical miracles. I've had it!"

With a bedside smile, my dear doctor looked at me and said simply, "We're keeping you alive, Bob. That's all I can say."

"Well, I don't believe it. When twenty people are in a small room, none of them knows what to do. When you've got twenty pills in your intestines, they don't know what the hell they're doin' either."

"We can cut down the dosage."

"Not good enough."

"Well, before we do anything radical I'm sending you to Cedars for an MRI of your brain."

"Well, at least that's proactive. Is tomorrow soon enough, Doc?"

Two days later I was lyin' on a slab, being rolled into a nuclear magnetic resonance imaging tunnel. Later in the day I was in Dr. Kivowitz's office. I pressed the good doctor to press the head of the Imaging Center to get an immediate result.

"You know, Evans, you really are a pain in the ass."

"Hope so. Make the call."

I was feeling cocky, knowing that I had made a resolution: no more twenty-pill days for Evans.

The MRI results came back. Scanning the page, "Well, Evans," said Dr. Kivowitz, "yes, there is damage from the stroke, which is inevitable and only to be expected. But, yes, it is correctable with a lot of work and training. It's not going to be easy, Evans, but it is doable and up to you how hard you try."

I looked at him straight. "Well, doctor, since I was a kid, the flair of the dare has always been my greatest enticement." I'm a guy who has always pushed the envelope. This time the glue was stronger, but did I stop fighting? Uh-uh. I fought harder—stupidly harder.

It's easy to say age is only numbers. Bullshit! The numbers catch up to you. They do to everyone. The bigger the ego, the less chance you think they have of catching you. But they do. And the higher the number, the harsher the pain.

Have my daredevil ways gotten me in trouble? Big-time! Has my road made others envious? It ain't been Yellow Brick, but I've seen a world of Oz that few others have ever done. Did I pay the price for it? Front-row center. But I don't believe in the past, and I don't believe in the future. I believe in the now. And I've paid the two dollars too many times to beat the system called life.

Next time around my MO will be POM—peace of mind.

One thing I've learned:

The fuckin' you get just ain't worth the fuckin' you get.

Late that year, my brother, Charles, invited me to join him on his boat in St. Barth's for the holidays.

I said no. The more I told him about my condition, the more he tried to encourage me. The more he tried to encourage me, the deeper my depression grew. His kind embrace was appreciated, but I knew I would envy his normal life too much to enjoy spending the holidays with him. Instead I spent the week in bed, alone, spending several hours a day working on my memoir, taking in the football games, and doing the excercises I hate.

Thus ended 1998, the worst year of my life.

The next day was New Year's Day. At two o'clock in the af-

ternoon, I called for my limousine. Instructions: destination unknown. Opening the door, my chauffeur, Stretch, asked politely
if I wanted a New Year's cocktail or the daily paper.

"Thanks but no thanks, Stretch." Instead I slipped him a Ben
Franklin. "Happy New Year, pal."

"Thank *you*, Mr. E. Where to?

"Anywhere between Santa Barbara and San Diego," I said.
"Find the most deserted, unknown beach. That's the destination."

He offered a comforting smile. "I know the coastline as well
as you know how to make a picture. I'll surprise you with the
most beautiful beach on the coast. It's New Year's Day and it's
cold. The beach will be all yours."

"You're my man, Stretch."

I pressed a button. The divider went up. Slowly my eyes closed,
and I fell into the deepest sleep I'd had in years.

A hand shook my arm. It was Stretch. "We're here, Mr. E."

"Where?"

"The beach I told you about. It's even more beautiful than I
remembered."

"Where are we?"

"Ten minutes from La Jolla."

"I must have slept for more than an hour!"

"You must've had one hell of a night last night. You feeling
better now?"

I nodded and got out of the car. Slowly my eyes spanned the
miles of beachfront before me. "What time is it?"

"Almost four thirty. Could have driven you all the way to San
Francisco and you wouldn't have opened your eyes."

• • •

Eerie, how even the slightest change of air can change your out-look on life. Out here, it hit me with a jolt: Weaknesses don't disappear, they just hang around waiting for their time at bat. I'd been in the house too long, seeing fewer and fewer people. Could agoraphobia have been setting in? Yeah! And I didn't like it.

"I'll be here waiting for you, Mr. E.," Stretch said.

"Why don't you go grab something to eat," I said. "Come back in an hour."

As he drove away, I slowly took off my shoes and hobbled down the steps, my feet touching the sand. The cold winter wind was going right through me, but I wasn't cold. I must have been dazed by the outside world.

When I got to the water, the last of the waves washed up and over my ankles. This time, I could feel it: The water *was* cold. It awakened my half-sleeping brain.

Was I dreaming it? No, I wasn't. Everything I was feeling was real. And I was part of it.

With a silent whisper, I begged for His embrace.

The impossible, I asked. *Is it possible?*

It was.

Just months later, as I was still working through my MRI chal-lenge, more enticing plans came into play.

The intercom buzzed.

"Jeff Berg on the phone, sir."

"I'm not here."

"He says it's urgent, Mr. Evans."

"I'm not here!"

No such luck.

An hour later, Jeff Berg walked right through my door like the captain of industry he was. In actuality he had been my good friend and agent for twenty-five years and a no-nonsense man if ever there was one.

"What are you doing here?"

"Saving your ass, that's what."

"Yeah, sure. Let me get back under the covers, will ya?"

Like a Marine sergeant he tore the sheets off the bed.

"Now listen and listen carefully. No more of this self-pity shit! I'm not here to get a commission!"

"A commission?" My first laugh of the day. "I've never paid you a dime in twenty-five years. You never wanted one. You were with me at the beginning. . . . Yeah, and you're with me at the end."

"That's where you're wrong, Evans! You've just struck football!"

Football? "What the fuck are you talking about?"

"Two hours ago I got the most bizarre call of the year. The top honcho of ESPN. I don't even know the guy. But he wants you!"

"Me?"

"That's right, you! ESPN has just bought the rights for *Sunday Night Football*. They're spending a fortune promoting it. It's a huge commitment for them. They're launching against the networks, so they have to launch big. And they've come up with an ingenious preseason promotional campaign. They're making the largest dollar commitment they've ever made—every station of every kind across the board. They're determined to make the public aware of their new flagship sports empire."

"What's that got to do with me?" I slurred.

"They want you to be the voice of ESPN *Sunday Night Football*, that's all!"

"Are you crazy? Jeff! That stroke left me with half a tongue! One half moves one way, the other half moves another. Sure, it's getting better. But the only thing I could promote audibly would be a freak show!"

Berg interrupted.

"Keep quiet and listen, will you? First of all, they don't know you had a stroke. The reason they want you is your fuckin' audio of *The Kid*. You're their first, second, and third choice to be the voice of ESPN's new sports breakthrough. You're doing this, Evans!"

"But Jeff, I can't."

". . . and you don't have to do it until late August, early September. You've got three months to prepare."

"Prepare, my ass! I got half a tongue! What's the other half gonna do?"

"Get better, that's what! How many hours a day do you spend on speech therapy?"

"Two to three hours, seven days a week. Is that enough?"

"No! Double it! You can do it! Anyway, it's too late. I committed you for it."

"But Jeff . . . !"

"There's no *buts*!"

If ever an aphorism fit the crime, this was it: When your back's against the wall, the impossible becomes possible.

For the next three months, I spent half my days slowly, painfully retraining the left half of my tongue to work in concert with the right. That one inch of flesh became the biggest hurdle of my life. The right side of my tongue . . . connecting with the left . . .

Think it's easy? Hah!

Post time was August 24. That gave me three months to start sounding like Orson Welles.

As I worked, Jeff negotiated. A whopper of a contract! Thanks, Jeff! But how was I gonna get the fuckin' words out of my mouth?

Progress, when it came, was excruciating. The deadline was looming.

I was sure I was going to make a fool of myself. The studio they were using to record was in Long Island. A few days before the recording date, on August 21, I went to my brother Charlie's in Quahog just a few minutes away, hoping to dispel my fears. But they only got worse.

On the appointed day every omen seemed against me. Walking into the recording studio, I found it was nothing more than a glorified shack filled with recording equipment, two booths, a few engineers, the director, and his assistant. They all greeted me and complimented me on the audio of *The Kid*. They had no idea what they were in for. As far as I knew, they would be hearing Elmer Fudd.

What happened next is on tape or I'd never get anybody to believe it.

What they wanted was no mere commercial. They'd scripted out the groundwork for an entire year's coverage: seventeen sixty-second monologues telling viewers what to expect from ESPN *Sunday Night Football*. They capsuled the entire football season in one afternoon. The financial offer I'd agreed to had sounded pretty good, but it was really slave labor. There must've been someone Up There looking out for me.

What transpired that afternoon overshadowed reality. No doctor and no therapist could've delivered the rounded tones that came out. I thought I was dreaming. It was akin to a mute breaking out with the Gettysburg Address.

Produced by Wieden+Kennedy, "My Guy," take one, August 19, 1998.

Generations of American boys have grown up playing with fully armed, fully posable action figures. When you were a kid and you played war with your friends, you would project yourself onto your action figure, you'd identify with him, you would send him on missions and refer to him as "my guy." "My guy" is gonna take out the machine-gun nest, "my guy" is gonna blow up the bridge, "my guy" is gonna liberate France.

This season, when you sit down to watch Sunday Night Football *on* ESPN, *think about that. Because when those two teams walk out onto the field, consciously or unconsciously, you will identify with one of them. Maybe it's their style, maybe it's because they're the underdogs, maybe you just like their helmets. Regardless, you'll identify with one of those teams. Who're you pulling for? Who do you identify with?*

Who's your guy?

ESPN Sunday Night Football—seventeen weeks, eighteen games.

Hey pal. Who's your guy?

"Vegas Preseason"

It's incredible what's happened to Vegas. Las Vegas used to be this sort of wicked city that was above the law. Then, practically overnight it became a "great place to take the family."

A twentieth-century man didn't need another "great place to take the family." He needed Vegas. Unfortunately, like almost everything meaningful and interesting, they took it away from us.

Well, this season, when you sit down to watch ESPN's Sunday Night Football, think about the value that final game of the weekend has in your life. It is the oasis in a wasteland of responsibility. The last-minute stay of execution. Daddy's quiet time. It's like some huge recalibration of the karmic scale, where Vegas is transformed into a sanitized theme park and Sunday night becomes a forum for a nationally televised, prime-time cockfight.

It almost makes up for Vegas.

They had scheduled three days for the recording. We finished in one afternoon. When it was over, the director and his hardened assistants stood and applauded! "We booked you for three days and you finished in five hours!"

He didn't know how right he was.

For the next several months, the campaign played on every AM and FM station imaginable, launching a flagship that was the network's mainstay for a decade. More people stopped me on the street and in restaurants to ask "Are you the guy from *Sunday Night Football*?" than had ever stopped me for anything I'd ever done before.

Do you believe in miracles? I do now.

When I came back home, ESPN wanted to make an exclusive contract with me. Jeff turned them down.

"Forget film!" he said. "Your voice on radio and TV can cover both your mortgages for the rest of your life. The crazy thing is, Evans . . . your tongue is the key to your fuck-you money!"

And, for the next several years, it was.

23

Adios to one miserable year. Hello to a better one!

There I stood, behind the regal gates of Paramount, ensconced in my primo offices of twenty-five years. The primo corner table at the studio commissary kept on constant reserve. Big-time high all the way.

That was the good news. The bad news? As I got more and more famous with a younger and younger crowd, my peers' resentments were becoming more painfully evident.

The studio was kind enough to spend a whopping ten thousand to option a comic how-to manual, *How to Lose a Guy in 10 Days,* and now it was going into preproduction—with Matthew McConaughey and Kate Hudson. Me? I'm seeing them smiles and embraces, but I'm wondering if they're all disguising one question:

Is this guy over-the-hill?

They'd find out soon enough.

By now, not only was my memoir, *The Kid Stays in the Picture*, climbing the bestseller list—but my audio book was achieving cult status. I had recorded it myself, before the strokes, insisting on taking more than a month to portray each of the characters.

The book and the audio exploded.

Suddenly, I'm throwing naturals. C'mon, seven, c'mon, eleven, let's go for it. And I did.

The book quickly received not only international bestseller status but critical acclaim throughout the world, and was published in a dozen languages. The irreverence of youth responded to my notoriety—to the point where it made me more a celebrity than a producer. I made considerable fees in speaking engagements in less than a year, while producers whose credits generated box-office gold went unrewarded and worse, unrecognized. For good reason: no one knows what a producer is or does, but everyone knew me. This was a double-edged sword if ever there was one.

The Kid was catching on, attracting the national media and capturing the attention of a younger generation. In *Details*, John Brodie published an article headlined "The Cult of Bob": "The current required reading has become *The Kid Stays in the Picture,* the actor-turned-producer's sordid and soaring autobiography . . . read by the great man himself. The audio version has caused a minor sensation. As a result, Evans has dethroned L. Ron Hubbard and Anthony Robbins as the maharishi of the moment for the generation who seem to long for a time when the studios made films—not merely theme park rides—and the town's social life was more akin to *Shampoo* than *The Firm*." Brodie's lengthy profile in *Details* was echoed by dozens of concurrent articles and interviews on a global scale. In "The Last Original," a four-page cover story in the Sunday Calendar section of the *Los Angeles Times*, Amy Wallace wrote that "Robert Evans has lived nine lives in Hollywood, not all of them charmed. Today he's a hero to junior moguls and the apparent model for the movie producer in *Wag the Dog*."

In the midst of all this, Bernie Brillstein, an old pal of mine and one of the directors of the Aspen Comedy Festival, invited me to perform at the renowned annual arts event.

"What the hell can I do there, Bernie? Limp?"

"Just read from your book, Bob. That's all you gotta do. You'll be a refreshing surprise for all the stand-up comics that'll be there."

"Who's gonna be there?"

"Jerry Seinfeld, Doc Simon, Ben Stiller, Mike Nichols, Martin Short . . ."

"Hold it. I've heard enough. Are you crazy? I thought you were my pal! It'd be one thing if you were asking me to compete in the Special Olympics. But if you think I'm going to make a fool of myself going toe-to-toe with these guys . . . ? That's kamikaze time."

"Trust my instincts, Bob. Will ya do it?"

"They may be your instincts, Bernie, but it's my ass! How many people do I have to make a fool of myself in front of?"

"About a thousand."

"All comics?"

"Most."

"I got it. You want me to be the intermission break between Ben Stiller and Mike Nichols."

"Wrong, Evans. I'm pleading with you for the third time! Do you know why? 'Cause I want you to know who you really are!"

I sat there in total confusion.

"Bernie, you've known me too long. You know just the right button to press. The bigger the dare, the bigger the turn-on. Rev up them engines."

To say I was reluctant to fly to Aspen would be an underplay. If you'd told me I would fly back from there a comedy sensation, I'd have thought you were on an acid trip. Thank heavens for the legitimacy of the printed word! No one would have believed what happened if it hadn't been headlined by the *Los Angeles Times* and *Variety*.

At the appointed hour, I bit the bullet and looked out at the stage.

I was following Martin Short, who was very tall in talent and very funny in delivery.

I had no idea what I would say.

I limped out and looked at the audience. In a moment of panic, or inspiration, I blurted:

"Ten months ago today I had a . . ."

. . . and my hand began to shake.

"I had a . . ."

I dropped my script and grabbed the podium and then the mike.

"I had a . . . stro-o-o-o-ke. . . ."

And with that I fell to the floor, holding the microphone in one hand, the script in the other.

The dignitaries in the front row jumped up and ran to the stage, yelling, "Emergency! Call nine-one-one!"

"I can't breathe . . . ," I gasped. "Can't breathe . . ."

The rush to the stage became general . . .

. . . and I started calmly reading from my book. From the floor.

Those around me tried to pick me up, but I brushed them away, rising with microphone in one hand and book in the other. As gracefully as I could, I walked to the plush chair and continued my reading—to a standing ovation.

Can't deny that, at my age, being discovered as the new comedy find of the year was like being discovered by Darryl Zanuck all over again.

Not too long afterward, Neil Simon asked me to dinner at the Palm.

"Evans, I must tell you, I've done a little comedy in my time, but I've never seen better comic timing in my entire career. That stroke put us all to shame. How'd you do it? Who worked with you on it?"

"Truth, Doc? When I walked out onstage, I didn't know I was going to do that at all. I didn't know what to do. So I just dropped dead instead of dying."

In the middle of the Palm restaurant, the great Neil Simon burst out laughing. "That's comedy, Kid."

I've always lived on impulse—impulse good, impulse bad. I'd

have to say, this was not only my most lunatic impulsive act, but the one that left me with the fondest memories.

The press, and the Internet, spread the word of my idiosyncratic performance—big-time. This time good. No, very good. Suddenly I was being booked on public speaking tours; there was talk of a one-man Broadway show called *In Bed with Robert Evans*. My doctors were against all of it, but that sounded like one helluva dare. Bernie was blowing smoke up my ass, trying to convince me that I could go with the best as a raconteur . . . and I was believing it. Bernie was a better salesman than a doctor and I was looking favorably on taking the dare.

My public speaking engagements made it very clear to me that walking into a room and limping into one are two different emotions. I could make my way across a floor, but I couldn't negotiate stairs. It was the one remaining hurdle to camouflage that I couldn't beat. As much as I practiced, hour after hour, I couldn't Fred Astaire an entrance or exit, up or down any stairs. Still can't.

Though I'd been blessed by the Guy Upstairs, He had left his mark.

For the first time, I began feeling old. My heavy-duty rehabilitation continued: I had to keep working on my limbs, every day, if I wanted to avoid being a gimp. For the first time I started feeling lonely—very lonely. Solitude and my cerebellum became close buddies. I didn't like the feeling, but I couldn't stop it.

It was like a cancer taking over my personality.

My vanity overshadowed my pragmatism. I kept making money as a public speaker, but in private . . .

When the millennium came, I spent the evening ringing in the new year—alone. For ten years I'd been looking forward to that moment. I'd made it . . . on the outside. On the inside, a different emotion prevailed. I started to hate my own self-pity. Though the year had been good to me, I was still a half-assed invalid. Not looked up to, but looked at. I didn't feel like Evans any more. Lack of agility gave me a lack of confidence; lack of confidence gave me a lack of social graces. They used to come naturally. Now they weren't coming at all.

Hope is the feeling you have that the feeling you have isn't permanent. Hope was fading fast.

Did I like myself? No. Did I like who I was becoming? No.

You didn't return my call, you snob."

"You're calling me a snob?" I burst out laughing. "That's a helluva compliment coming from the world champ. Thanks for being here, Graydon."

"Thanks for not inviting me."

For an hour we laughed, talked, reminisced.

Graydon Carter stood tall in my life—among the tallest. Forget the fact that for more than twenty years he's been editor in chief of *Vanity Fair*. Forget the fact that he's the hottest ticket in our town wherever and whenever he arrives. What's more important is that during the worst of my trials, when I was looked upon with total disfavor, Woodland was always his first stop when arriving in Flicksville.

Here's a guy who needs me zero, and he's one of the very few in my life who's gone out of his way to be there for me at my lowest. Here's a guy who throws the year's hottest Hollywood party of the year, every year . . . and he's here at Woodland three hours before it starts.

Together we walked toward the projection room. I couldn't help but think how insensitive my behavior'd been. Not only had I failed to send him a thank-you note after he'd come to the hospital three times and been turned away, but since I returned to Woodland I hadn't even had the courtesy to place a call to let him know I was still breathing . . . well, sort of. Or to RSVP for his Oscar party. And this was one of the most sought-after men in the world, one who had stayed by my side through thin and thin.

"Coffee and a scone, Graydon?"

"Just coffee."

Dialing the kitchen, I ordered two coffees, "down and dirty." A Carter laugh.

I couldn't help but stare at him. Graydon was tan; his eyes and smile glowed.

"Get dressed, Evans!"

"Thanks but no thanks, Graydon. I'm not up for the room."

"The room is lucky to have you."

"I don't even have a date!"

"I'm your date."

"I don't wanna go, Graydon. Please don't make me."

He laughed. "You have no choice. You're walking in with me."

"I don't even have the right clothes! I don't have a tuxedo!"

"Turn-downs are not accepted. Especially from you. You're walking in with me, and that's it."

The party was due to start at five. Finally, I gave in and headed off to put myself together.

Graydon stood there beside me. "Okay, where's your closet?"

And he stayed there with me, helping me get dressed, until I was ready. I don't think I could have put myself together if he hadn't been there beside me. Buttoning my shirt, tying my tie, actually helping me get into my shoes and tying the laces.

"Just one favor, though, Evans?"

"What is it?"

"Don't tell anyone I'm your valet."

What happened that night was the turning point of my life.

Sitting beside Graydon that night at the primo round table at Morton's was dreamlike. Not *good* dreamlike, just dreamlike.

On one side of me was Graydon's boss, Si Newhouse, the owner of Condé Nast. Next to him were Barry Diller, who owned the USA Network at that time, and the record mogul David Geffen. Graydon stood up and made a toast.

"To the Kid," he said. When he sat down, he kissed me on the cheek and smiled. "Be at your house tomorrow at noon."

At the stroke of twelve, there stood Graydon. Walking to the projection room, he laughed. "It must have been a year and a half ago, right before your stroke, you came to my apartment and asked if I'd give a look-see to a manuscript you were working on. I said I would—if you came to a party with me on Saturday night. Matthew Tyrnauer was having his thirtieth birthday at the Mercer hotel. At first you didn't want to go. . . ."

"Yeah, I remember wondering, *What the hell am I going to do there? Everyone will be under thirty. I'll feel like an ogre.*"

Was I wrong! Entering the Mercer hotel that evening in March 1998 was the most startling lesson in how tilted one person's subjective view of himself can be. It was among the most shocking evenings of my life.

I walked into a room filled with bright young men and women in their twenties and thirties, feeling like Grampa Evans—and left four hours later knowing that my irreverent road through life had left its dent with generations far younger.

Graydon left the party two hours before. Me? I couldn't get out. They wouldn't let me. Birthday Boy Matt came over and embraced me. "You made my party, Evans. Thanks for being here."

"Matt! Best party I've ever been to, kid. It may have been your birthday, but it was my coming-out party."

Totally dazed, I walked from the Mercer to the Carlyle. Felt like the longest walk of my life.

Now, Carter and I stood together by the pool.

"Graydon, I'm one lucky motherfucker having you in my life."

Laughing: "You're damn right you are! You're a strange phenomenon, Evans. You're almost mythical. Just by doing nothing, you multiply your persona by ten. That's who you are today! That's why I want to make the movie. Imagine—since the night of Tyrnauer's party, you've had three strokes, flatlined, and come back to life! You pitch me a better movie and I'll make it!"

Thus began the greatest odyssey of my life

Behind my desk at Paramount, 2000.

A great birthday night for my ageless boss, Sumner Redstone.

Alan Berliner

An affectionate moment with the
extraordinary Beverly D'Angelo.
Alan Selka

Teaching the young John McEnroe a bit of tennis in *Players*, a flick about Wimbledon.

Giving tennis lessons to the world's top tennis player, Novak Djokovic, at Woodland.

Alan Selka

With Slash and Jeff Danna,
signing DVDs of my movie.
Alex "Rio" Bier

Presenting awards to my
pals Snoop Dogg and 50 Cent
at the Vibe Awards.
Getty

With P. Diddy and Francis Coppola on Ron Perelman's yacht,
New Year's Eve, 2004.

Tatijana Shoan

Enjoying an industry party with Serena Williams.

Brett Ratner

A generous gesture from my dear friend Helmut Newton.

Helmut Newton

My close friends Helmut and June Newton,
watching a film in my projection room.

Alan Selka

I kissed him good-night. He kissed me good-bye. Outside the Palm restaurant
on the night before dear Helmut's unexpected death.

Brett Ratner

Getting the prizewinning laugh at the Aspen Comedy Festival.

Alan Selka

What a way to wish upon a star.

Alex "Rio" Bier

At a Mike Tyson fight
at Caesar's Palace with
Margaux Hemingway.

With Warren Beatty and Michael Jackson at Woodland.

Brett Ratner

Great ad sabotaged by
misinformation. It played on
Tuesday, not Wednesday!

Jennifer Howard Kessler

Me and my shadow,
Kid Notorious.

Receiving the David O. Selznick Award
from the Producers Guild of America,
with Dustin Hoffman looking on.
Alan Berliner

At Woodland with Joshua and Jackson: three generations of Evanses.

Meeting with Patrick Milling Smith, producer of the Tony Award–winning
phenomenon *Once*, to discuss bringing *The Kid* to Broadway.

Alex Koester, New York Times

Woodland, inside and out.

Addressing a Q&A session at the opening of the new
Soho House theater on Sunset Boulevard.

The next day, the phone rang. "Graydon Carter, sir."

I picked up.

"Bob? I just closed the quickest deal of my career. I called Barry Diller and told him, 'Barry, you heard what I said the other night? I toasted to it, and you're my first call. I'm totally committed to making *The Kid Stays in the Picture* as a film. Would you like to do it with me?' Diller didn't skip a beat. 'You have a deal. Is that a quick enough answer? Let's not even discuss the finances.'"

Even Graydon's cool voice cracked. "Bob, it's the quickest deal I've ever made. Exciting, isn't it?"

Sure it was. But for some reason I was the least excited of all. The next day I called Graydon's chosen directors, Brett Morgen and Nanette Burstein, to talk over the news. We sat down for our first meeting of what to put on the screen. That's when the drama started.

To begin with, to make the film the way we wanted, we would have to get releases from everyone appearing in the film—from the biggest stars to the most powerful and reclusive characters who played a part in my bumpy road. Of the 256 people who appeared onscreen, 255 signed on.

Me? I hated the thought of making the film. I was impossible to work with.

My first and foremost demand was one that, if I were the producer, would've been reason enough to close the production down:

I would do the voice-over. But I would not appear in a single frame of the film.

Brett looked at me as if I were crazy.

"How can we make a picture of you without you in it? You're not the Shadow!"

"Oh yes I am."

"So tell me, Mr. Thalberg, how do we make the picture?"

"I've been on camera since I was fifteen. There's more film on me than Cartier has diamonds."

"Yeah, but Cartier has diamonds."

"Well, they're a girl's best friend, aren't they? Film on me is gonna have to become your best friend. Anyway, you can walk or I can walk, any way you want it. Either way, it's a deal breaker."

"Graydon didn't tell us this."

"Graydon doesn't know it yet. My voice you got, my face you don't. And do you know, Brett? You could make it work."

The search began.

The first thing we had to do was review the libraries of film upon film upon film of me. The good news was, the camera was never shy to me. My seemingly cavalier life always seemed to interest Mr. Kodak. The bad news was, this gave us huge amounts of material to review. Conversely, it took us a good six to eight months to realize that we had two problems: Not only would it cost a potential fortune to use the voluminous amount of film we needed, it would also involve asking people to appear as themselves in another's alarming story. But Brett and Nanette and their talented assistants, plus Graydon's singular power of persuasion, made it possible for all the elements we needed to fall into place. None of it could have happened without their specific expertise.

Documentaries are usually made about people who are dead, though no one pointed that out to me at the time. I wouldn't have been shocked if my filmmakers had thought they were in for such a scenario with me. Yeah, but they needed my voice. From a pragmatic point of view, this was my insurance policy. They kept me in filmland's ICU till our story's last frame was put to bed. Finding matching footage and scoring haunting music, they were racing for the finish line—specifically, opening night at Sundance's premiere theater.

Did we make it?

My professional instincts had warned me it would be a disaster. I'd fought with everybody for two years, was embarrassed by many parts, felt raped by the things that were exposed on the screen—you name it, I shuddered at revealing it.

Did it work? I wouldn't know till we got to the last ten minutes. Instead of standing in the back of the theater enjoying the hilarity of its play, I was in a cold sweat. Only doom crossed my mind.

Would it work? The screen turned to black. I actually did not know where I was standing.

In unison, the entire audience stood. I knew I was dreaming it. The applause began, and unlike any other film I've ever been involved with, instead of reaching a crescendo, the applause grew louder. Young filmmakers started to shout my name.

The film was a cinematic shocker, not merely a documentary but a new form of drama that left the jaded audience of Sundance spellbound.

Brett Morgen pushed me forward.

"You hear that? It's for you, you schmuck. Now go out there and give it to 'em." In his eyes he had tears of joy.

Only one who'd been doomed to die in the chair at the Big House could have experienced the jolt of electricity that shot through me. Not being Fred Astaire, but rather a born-again cripple, I fell on the stairs on the way up to the stage. When I got up and stood there, looking out at the audience, my face was totally expressionless.

From the middle of the theater, a young man's voice yelled out: "How does it feel, Mr. Evans?"

The applause swelled further.

"How does it feel?" the young man yelled again. "Tell us!"

Scanning the audience, I called it what it was.

"It's the second time in my life that I've actually hallucinated." The laughter hit high.

"It's the truth. The first time was with Cary Grant."

Cary Grant and me: That was quite a story.

• • •

The late Cary Grant was considered the ultimate charmer by all who crossed his path. He was charm with a capital *C*.

In the late fifties, incident brought together Mr. Movie Star and Mr. Wannabe. The incident? A young Yugoslavian basketball player. No, not a guy! A five-foot, eleven-inch hunk of woman who was all but an exact replica of Sophia Loren. Her name? Luba Otashavich.

She was Cary's protégée but at the same time she became my lady fair. Grant and I shared one lady and one thought. We both knew it was not platonic, on either side. That's one hell of a way to start a friendship. But it did—big!

One day he called us together. "Dear Luba, Bob, I'm going to let you in on a big secret. It will be out next month on the cover of *Look*. I'm the first celebrated person who admits his dependency. I am addicted to LSD, though only under a doctor's care.

"It's changed my life and I want you both to experience its transformational power—only once, as a token of togetherness. You must promise me beforehand that it will be your last and only time. As your mentor, I insist that you make the experience singular. One time and one time only. Do you promise? It's a weakness of mine, but it should be a source of strength to you both never to use it again."

That Saturday morning the three of us lay back on our separate chairs. The doctor put one blue pill on Cary's tongue, one on Luba's, and one on mine.

And do you know what happened? I hallucinated.

That was almost fifty years ago, and I've wanted to repeat the process many a time . . . but I haven't. That is, until tonight— and this time I didn't need the pill. I kept my promise to you, dear Cary. Wherever you are tonight, Cary, this time it's all natural.

And thus began the most celebrated years of my entire career.

Once again, Graydon's vision was on the nose. His choice of Brett and Nanette as directors was instinctively acute. As producer, he knew the right buttons to push to get the right film from the right people. If ever a whole was greater than the sum of its parts . . . It was a tribute to narrative structure, to the magic of film. What vision it took to imagine that the scattered bits of another's life could render a compelling drama that could bring tears, and laughter—and even, yes, joy to the viewer.

That night at Sundance, Graydon came up with the idea of using the theater at Woodland—itself a character in the drama—to unveil his latest production for a select group of opinion-makers: twenty-two people per evening for ten successive evenings.

As usual for Graydon, it became the toughest ticket in town.

He did the inviting, except for the two opening-night tickets I held back—for Jack and Warren. That night, I introduced the film, then sneaked back to my bedroom while the audience watched in the screening room. When it ended I looked out my window and watched the audience filing out. But no Jack and Warren; they'd sneaked out to knock on my bedroom door, which was locked.

When I opened the door, they both embraced me. I actually thought I saw a tear in Warren's eye. No, that couldn't be.

Jack hugged me, smiled wide. "Keed, we are so proud of you. The picture ain't good, it's great."

Warren interrupted. "Can't believe you pulled it off. You even made us actors look good."

The three of us hugged. Those five minutes together were more than worth the two years I'd spent undressing myself emotionally for the world to see. In that moment, there was no one in the world wealthier than me.

The film opened at Cannes the following month. It was entered into the festival as a special attraction. Graydon pulled out every stop imaginable at the Hotel du Cap, hosting a premiere party for four hundred people.

As I was getting ready to leave for Cannes, though, what do you think happened? *Wham! Bam!* Stage fright plus! I just couldn't face the music, much as I wanted to go. I thought I was ready for everything. . . . Wrong! I couldn't face the biggest night of my life. There I lay, half-assed, discombobulated

both mentally and physically. Four hundred international luminaries had flown around the world to attend Graydon's gala.
Excuse me, three hundred and ninety-nine. I was looking like
a no-show.

Graydon was furious, and rightly so. But my problem was simple: I couldn't move.

It was too late to cancel the party; the showing was in two
days. Brett Morgen called from Cannes. "Evans! You gotta be
here. We're not allowed to walk the red carpet without you! Don't
do this to me!"

Jeff Berg of ICM grabbed the phone. "Listen carefully, Evans.
You've become a bigger diva than Marilyn Monroe! I don't want
to hear about any of your cockamamie neuroses! If you're a no-
show, forget my name and move to Palm Springs!"

I didn't make the party, though Brett Morgen called me from
the event to wish me well.

What could I do? I called Nicholson.

Miraculously, he was flying to Cannes for his picture, *About
Schmidt*. He was leaving the next afternoon on a private plane to
the festival. I told him my dilemma.

"No problem, Keed. I'll take you on my plane. It won't be the
biggest, but it'll be the best. You deserve it. You gotta be there.
Call Graydon and tell him you're flying in for the showing, with
me by your side. I'll have a car pick you up."

And that's just what happened.

By the time I got to Cannes, I may not have been at my best—
but I made the red carpet the next day, and I got a more enthusiastic response than any of my pictures ever had at Cannes.
The picture received a prolonged standing ovation, rare for the

festival and certainly unexpected by me. And the one who was applauding most was Barry Diller, the man standing next to Graydon, who'd given the film the quickest thumbs-up of his whole career.

As we headed to the after-party, I kept saying to myself, *How could I have missed that party? How could I have missed all this? I must be really sick—in the head.*

From there we traveled to Deauville for the festival there, where I received another award. Holding up the statue, I was in French seventh heaven. *This can't be happening to me*, I thought. *I'm doing better in my second life than in my first.* On we went to Paris, where I was treated with far more respect and celebrity than I had been thirty years before, when I'd hosted the presidential premiere of *The Godfather* at the Opera, a rare occurrence for any film. My date that evening had been Romy Schneider, my company the Pompidous and the Rothschilds. This time? The excitement of Cannes and Deauville had transformed me from over-the-hill filmmaker into an international film icon.

Suddenly the Kid became the darling of the European circuit, and off to London we went for the black-tie premiere at the Odeon, Leicester Square. At the post-premiere party, the topic of conversation was Graydon's introduction of the film.

"I have spent so much time with this subject," he said, "that when I die, Robert Evans's life is going to flash before my eyes!"

How exciting the time! And how exhausting! Its first weekend, opening in limited release in New York and Los Angeles, saw *The Kid* tops in per-screen average—better than any other film at that time. The quote from *Variety*'s front page?

"Bio doc reaping an incredible $22K/venue, the best per-theater average for any specialty title to date this summer." Sounds good, huh?

Me? I was ecstatic—momentarily, at least.

"We've got ourselves a mini-blockbuster," echoed Graydon.

D arling, whose bed do you think I'm on? Take a guess. At the moment I'm lying on a mink bedspread and I'm being served a cheese soufflé. I only wish you were here to have it with me."

Laughing into the phone.

"That's right, I'm at Evans's. In ten minutes we're watching the Lewis/Tyson fight. It's on HBO and I forgot to order it. Talk to you after the fight."

It was Warren Beatty, speaking to his better half, Annette Bening, who was on location shooting a film.

Shaking my head. "What a gal."

"Only the best," he smiled back. "Who do you like in the fight?"

"It's a tough call."

"That's why I asked. They're both over-the-hill, both great fighters. One is just slightly further over-the-hill than the other. It makes a difference. Age catches up to you."

"It sure does."

The fight started. Both fighters looked lethargic.

"Told you—age catches up."

Round two was no better. "Five years ago it would've been a brawl."

"Speaking of brawls," I said, "who's the oldest above-the-line star you ever balled?"

I had just broken the unspoken rule Warren and I had shared for decades: never to ask about one another's amours unless they were widely known by the public—and, even then, when it came to the intricacies of the relationship, no questions asked.

Our reason? We feared the disillusionment of discovering that we'd been brothers-in-law too many times over. Underneath it all we had the same emotion—*don't ask . . . you don't want to know*—and we lived by that. Continued silence is the greatest insurance policy for continued friendship. And it worked.

Until now. Suddenly, Warren turned the DA act on me.

"Who's the oldest above-the-line diva *you* ever balled?"

We both burst out laughing as round four began. The fight was getting interesting. For the next few rounds, we concentrated on the action.

Finally, Warren said, "Maybe it's true. Age is only numbers." Then he DA'd me again. "Come on. Give me the last initial of the last name and I bet I can guess who it is."

I quickly responded, "*You* give *me* the last initial and I bet I can guess."

The seventh round drew to a close. A minute into the eighth round, Lewis flattened Tyson, bringing the fight—and our little sparring match—to an end. To this day there's been no rematch between Lewis and Tyson, nor for that matter between Warren and the Kid.

Do I remember who the diva was? You bet your ass I do! But it's for no one to know, including the reader. However, the story itself has gotten me out of many a depression with a smile.

The year? Nineteen fifty-eight.

Flying back then was pre-jet, mucho luxury, and comfortably slower. TWA's red-eye was no red-eye. Three times a week, the airline had a flight from Los Angeles to New York at 11 P.M., landing in New York at 7 A.M. the following day. The tail of the plane consisted of six sleeping berths: three upper and three lower. Behind that was a small bar serving champagne and hors d'oeuvres—a luxury afforded to only the select.

At that moment I was one of the chosen, flying in to New York for the premiere of my first costarring role, in *The Sun Also Rises*. Playing opposite Ava Gardner didn't do me any harm. For five minutes I was considered Twentieth Century Fox's new hot property—hence my spot among the other five notables on TWA's super-deluxe flight.

All six berths were occupied. One by my mentor Darryl Zanuck, head of Twentieth Century Fox and producer of *The Sun Also Rises*. Another by Walter Winchell, America's most dangerous and influential journalist. His 1,400-station, 1,000-newspaper reach could make or break any career in politics, show business, or industry. No one today can touch his influence. And he was one vengeful mother, always on the prowl for the next scandalous headline.

Peter Viertel, the author and friend of Hemingway's who'd written the screenplay for the film, was also on the flight. As was an over-the-hill blond movie diva who'd been famous worldwide for decades. And the starlet who broke his virginity in lush flying: me.

Once the plane was in the air and we were in the clouds, we were given our assigned berths. The lower berths were the most comfortable. Naturally, I was in a middle upper. Below me was the movie diva. Twenty-four inches across from her, the feared Winchell.

As night fell, an arm with a bejeweled hand crept up from the lower berth. Was I dreaming it? No. But I sure as hell was scared. Is this what goes on in Hollywood? What am I supposed to do?

Her fingers beckoned. I peeked out the curtain. Everything was dark. Winchell's berth was curtained in. Impulse overcame prudence. I took her hand, gesturing for her to climb up. She pulled back, beckoning me to come down. Call it a seductive tug-of-war if you wish, but who was I to be demanding? I quickly peeked out again and the flair of the dare made a midair affair—two feet from the most dangerous man in the country, who could ruin my career forever—an irresistible proposition.

For Walter Winchell to be twenty-four inches from the sex scandal of the year . . . and sleep through it? Who could resist such a suicidal liaison?

I stealthily slipped down the few feet needed to enter her airborne boudoir. What happened is not for me to say, except for this: When I crept back to my upper berth my heart was pumping through my chest, not from the sexual experience, but from the knowledge that danger, especially when it's potentially lethal, is one hell of an aphrodisiac. And this was potentially fatal-plus.

The next morning, totally unknowing, Winchell approached me with a wide smile, shook my hand.

"Very glad to have met you. You're going to go far, young man."

I wanted to say *I did, Mr. Winchell,* but I kept my mouth shut. Thinking *If he only knew* was far more exciting than anything I could say.

Who the lady was, no one will ever know—including Warren.

S plashed across the front page of the *Wall Street Journal* of October 24, 2002, was the biggest surprise of my print career. Me on the front page of the *Journal?* With one of those engraved portraits usually reserved for the captains of industry? But no captain of industry was I—rather, a pirate of broken rules who'd paid the consequences of his own more-than-cavalier life.

Written by one of their aces, Bruce Orwall, the article detailed the next chapter in my bumpy road: *Kid Notorious*, a cartoon series.

"On a late summer afternoon, Woodland, the estate of the legendary film producer Robert Evans, was infused with the feeling that anything can happen here.

"Former Guns N' Roses guitarist Slash strolled by the pool. MTV Networks Chairman Tom Freston arrived in tennis togs, heading for a lesson on the court out back. And as the 72-year-old Mr. Evans greeted visitors for lunch, he was interrupted by a striking young blond woman dressed in a red cashmere bathrobe. She gave Mr. Evans a languorous kiss.

"Life, it appears, is good for Mr. Evans, the former Paramount Pictures chief who in the 1970s brought films including *The Godfather* and *Chinatown* to the big screen.

"Until recently he was still battling the hangover from the brutal 20-year run in which he was virtually driven from the film business and laid low by a series of strokes.

"Today, he is in the midst of an improbable comeback. That's mainly because of the overwhelming response from show-business insiders to *The Kid Stays in the Picture*, a new documentary film based on Mr. Evans' tell-all 1994 book of the same name. The film, narrated by Mr. Evans in a seductive baritone, paints him as a smooth-talking, fast-living, skirt-chasing Hollywood maverick of the kind that has largely vanished since major corporations took control of the movie business.

"The result: Robert Evans, washed-up mogul, has been reborn as Robert Evans, living symbol of a time when Hollywood was a lot more fun. He's at work on a sequel to his book, dictating it in all-night sessions to an assistant from his bed. Comedy Central recently won a bidding war to develop an animated series about the semi-real adventures of Mr. Evans, his butler and his cat. The Producers Guild of America plans to give him its David O. Selznick Lifetime Achievement Award at a ceremony next spring, honoring him as 'one of the most vital and passionate advocates of our craft.'

"Mr. Evans' informal family—[including] his butler, Alan Selka; and *Kid* co-director Brett Morgen—were all on hand at Woodland recently to help him nail down what may be the biggest of the opportunities he is chasing. On that day, a half-dozen cable and TV networks angled for the opportunity to produce a cartoon series about him.

"Unlike most TV pitch sessions, which take place in sterile studio offices, the idea this time was to parachute the executives directly into Mr. Evans' world. 'They stepped into the cartoon,' says Mr. Selka, a veteran butler who says his outlook as a 'devout surrealist' has served him well during his 10 years with Mr. Evans. Dressed in a formal suit each day, Mr. Selka is so perfect for the his role that he is slated to do the voice-over work for his character in the cartoon series. 'I'm the straight man, so to speak,' he says.

"The pitch meetings were carefully scripted. Each group of executives was greeted at the door by Mr. Selka, who gave a tour of the house and grounds. Then the executives would meet with Mr. Morgen and executive producer Pam Brady in the pool house that Mr. Evans uses as a screening room. Mr. Evans would make an appearance near the meeting's end. While one network was in the meeting, the next group would tour the estate. 'We like them to run into each other,' Mr. Morgen said.

"A bidding war broke out, with Comedy Central and TNN vying hardest to land the show. In the end, Mr. Evans made a deal with Comedy Central."

What started out being potentially the greatest celebrative coup of my career ended being far more contentious than any of my divorces. Little did I know that the series' original title, "Pussy Power," was a dramatic foreshadowing of what awaited me.

For the next several months, I labored with a lot of talented people to put together what was considered one of the most innovative, intelligent, and funny cartoons ever aired on television. Comedy Central backed us with an advertising campaign that cost more than I spent publicizing *Chinatown*.

The result? Let the reviews speak for themselves:

Los Angeles Times: "It is Evans' own weird charm, which radiates through his low, lightly graveled voice, that makes the show work."

New York Post: "*Kid Notorious* is the drop-dead-funny new animated series on Comedy Central! Four stars!"

Bravo Online: "The show of the month!"

There were more. Reviews on a par with any of my films. And for an animated comedy? Doesn't seem possible, but fact's fact and that's a fact. High is high, and no one was higher than this Don Quixote. How could an animated cartoon meet with a critical embrace that none of my films had received in many a year? Sad but true.

But clouds were gathering . . . and they were jet-black.

"Creative differences" is a phrase Hollywood uses to describe the murderous hatreds, ferocious fights, and terrible misunderstandings that occur when too many supposedly creative people are put in the same place. The real culprit? Too many egos, including mine. Before we even hit our stride, "differences" began to arise between some of the people responsible for *The Kid Stays in the Picture* and the people of *Kid Notorious*. Being the Kid, I had to choose between them. Since my mantra has always been loyalty, I backed my original team for *The Kid Stays in the Picture*, who could no longer work with the *Kid Notorious* people. Where would I have been without them?

I let it be known that I could not support some of the creative team from *Kid Notorious*. In the blink of an eye, one of the writers on the show—a very talented woman I liked a lot—got the ax.

The payback was swift. I felt like the new girl in town who gets a date on Friday and the guy flips for her. The next night, same deal. Monday night? No one calls. Kid who? Despite its burgeoning cult status, *Kid Notorious* was relegated to the scrapheap of one-year wonders. By acting on those infamous "creative differences," I had inadvertently put a spike through my own heart.

Media coverage and audience appreciation are a rare combination—especially for a sophisticated, racy comedy with all the signs of a decade of staying power. What an idiot I was not to be a team player. You can't fight city hall and you can't fight the front office. If I'd used my brain and not my ego, *Kid Notorious* could still be on today. This half-hour interlude of cable cartoon is a constant reminder that you gotta play ball with the guy who owns the team—that's if you want to bat again. Instead of the home run I thought I was hitting, I struck out. I never got up to bat again. Damn it! I loved that show and the characters in it. I had more personal response from this supposedly insignificant half-hour show than almost any picture I've ever made. Does it bother me? You bet your ass it does! Who am I angry at? Not Comedy Central but yours truly.

Each day, when I awake, I'm reminded of one of the dearest friendships of my life. On the wall opposite my bed hangs my favorite piece of art in my collection: a six-foot-by-four-foot photographic image of two of my secretaries, nude and entwined, under a two-hundred-year-old sycamore tree in my garden. The photographer titled the piece *Lunch Break*. Across the bottom he inscribed it, in thick blue crayon: "for my friend, Robert Evans—Helmut Newton, Beverly Hills 1991 'In Robert's Garden.'"

In the many lectures I've given around the globe about the world of film, the one question I get asked most is: Who are the most talented people you've worked with? My response is always the same: I've worked with many who have touched brilliance, but there is only one I consider a genius. It's Helmut Newton. He is the true master of the still frame, who elevated the art of photography to the heights that make it the dominant art form of the twenty-first century.

In the fifties, Helmut's work was considered scandalous. In the sixties, it was considered provocative. By the seventies, he was recognized as a master. My opinion of Helmut's genius does not stand alone. Every major European nation bid for his archive, culminating in the building of the Helmut Newton museum in no less than the center of Berlin. Imagine: He is the first artist of photography to have a major museum devoted to his master works, thus breaking new barriers for the genre. The fact that Helmut took hundreds of portraits of me was not necessarily a compliment. "Bobby," he'd say, "you have a regal decadence in your facial bone structure that I cannot find in anyone else."

I threw many parties for Helmut and wife June Newton over the years, and soon came to realize that it was folly to invite anyone more than two days before the event. He had a greater allure than anyone I knew. His draw was so powerful that, as soon as word of a new party leaked, I would have needed the National Guard for crowd control. Girls wanted to meet Helmut more than anyone else, hoping to be immortalized by his infamous lens.

Not too many years ago, I gave a Christmas bash in my new offices at Paramount. What a turnout! More above-the-title flick stars filled the suite than cumulatively graced the studio all year. Helmut showed up late—yeah, but not too late. Them macho male sex stars? They faded into the background quicker than love at first sight. Not them ladies. They pitter-pattered into the foreground. All of them—from Movie Star to Ms. Society. All of 'em vying to get Helmut's eye.

Helmut was my hero. Gave guys like me, carrying far lower numbers, the shot of adrenaline we needed. With Helmut, I was suddenly a juvenile again, looking for danger. And I wasn't the only one: Just as many guys as dames were looking to meet him. Some of them were looking for the kink in his armor. They knew all about him, they thought, and they didn't like what they knew. Women? That was a different story. They didn't feign their attraction to him. When he was nearby, their headlights were always on high. Every one of them wanted to meet up with him, big. Get to know him better. Be dominated by his whims.

On the twenty-second of January 2004, my lady and I went out for dinner with Helmut and June. As we were leaving the Palm, a photographer caught me kissing Helmut good night. It turned out to be our last good-bye. The next morning, news of Helmut's death flashed across television screens. What seemed like just moments later, June, his extraordinary love and collaborator of fifty-four years, had me on the horn. "I know Helmut would want me to call . . . to tell you he beat you to the barn." Then, softly, she added: "No one loved you more than Helmut."

Well, dear Helmut, no one loved you more than I.

There have been many novels written about Hollywood, but only one has been hailed as legendary . . . and it wasn't even complete.

Of all the personalities who shaped film and the way films get made, of all the promoters and hustlers and part-time geniuses who've labored over scripts and schedules, lenses and releases, distribution and publicity—in other words, producers—only one has had the constellation of talents and circumstances to have affected not only his peers but generations of filmmakers to come. He was the subject of that legendary novel by F. Scott Fitzgerald: *The Last Tycoon*. In the book, the producer was named Monroe Stahr.

In real life, he was named Irving Thalberg.

At the age of twenty, Thalberg was head of production at Universal Studios—smart enough to run the studio, too young to sign the checks. It does sound like fiction, doesn't it? His life does, too—that's why Fitzgerald wrote it as a novel. *The Last Tycoon* remains the only incomplete novel that belongs in literature's hall of fame.

Despite the many changes in the film industry since Thalberg reigned in the twenties and thirties, he remains the beau ideal of Hollywood producers. No career has ever approached his. He oversaw dozens of productions a year personally, as well as overseeing, okaying, rewriting, reshooting, and reediting dozens more. He was married to Norma Shearer, one of the smartest and most glamorous actresses of her day, who won the second Academy Award ever bestowed.

Thalberg's talent was mythical. After his sudden death from a heart attack in 1937, no one ever filled the immense void he left. And so the Irving Thalberg Lifetime Achievement Award became the most coveted and the most prestigious award a producer can receive.

Imagine, then, how I felt when, in my mid-twenties, I was waved over to the side of the pool at the Beverly Hills Hotel by none other than Ms. Shearer herself.

"Are you an actor?"

"I'm not, but I used to be."

"Watching you by the pool, I said to Martin [Arrouge, her husband], 'That young man reminds me of Irving.' They're making *Man of a Thousand Faces* at Universal. It's about Lon Chaney. Irving played a very important part in Lon's life. Jimmy Cagney is playing Lon Chaney. They've sent fourteen actors for me to see and you're the first one who actually reminds me of the real Irving."

She sent me to meet the producer and director of the film. Against their professional wishes and to everyone's shock, I got the part. In December 1956, we started shooting.

My first day was nearly my last. Before the cameras rolled, Norma told me that Irving would never wear makeup, so she wanted me not to wear makeup. In my naïveté, I agreed. Not my last mistake.

The first thing they told me on the set? "Makeup!"

"But Ms. Shearer said I shouldn't wear makeup," I protested.

The director brooked no protests. "Makeup!"

Humbly, the new guy went along.

My father and brother flew out to Hollywood to watch me shoot with the great James Cagney, who had greeted me warmly. Lights, camera, roll sound, action . . . and nothing. The first line was mine; I had rehearsed it without incident. Now that the moment had arrived, I couldn't get a sound out of my mouth. Nothing.

Take two. Lights, camera, roll sound, action . . . nothing.

Never mind. Take three. Take four. Lights, camera . . . nothing. Not a syllable.

By now more people had gathered. An anxious stillness. I could hear muttering from behind the camera. Assistants were sent to fetch things; a cloud of unease fell over the set.

I could see the producer talking to the director.

Take five. Lights . . . my throat seized up completely. I couldn't even squawk, much less deliver a line. I started wondering how fast I could get out of town. Are there flights to New York tonight? By now the makeup team was patting me down.

One more try.

Lights, camera, roll sound, action . . . hopeless. I'd become the Sphinx, a tomb, a statue. I'd reverted to infancy. I couldn't make a sound.

I saw the great Cagney get up from his seat. *This is it*, I thought. *I had my shot . . . and I blew it.*

Cagney walked over to the director, whispered in his ear.

"All right, let's all take five!"

Cagney walked over to me. I was paralyzed with humiliation. He took me by the arm and guided me off the set. We walked outside, my legs trembling.

"Kid, on the first day of my first film, I had to do a scene with a guy who was six foot four. I'm five foot five. It was my job to bully the guy. Well, by the time the scene was over, I was six foot four and he was five foot five. Remember one thing, kid, in life and in acting: Don't be afraid. Not of me, not of anybody.

"Now, c'mon, let's go back on the set and show 'em good."

Imagine Jimmy Cagney saying that to me! He made me feel ten feet tall. Those words stayed with me for the rest of my life.

The next take was a print. I never had a problem like that again.

Of course, that didn't solve my makeup problem. On the first showing of dailies, Norma Shearer stood up the moment I came on screen, walked over to me, and said, *"I told you no makeup!"* Then she stomped out of the room. It took the director, the producer, and myself days to convince her that no makeup was just not possible.

The picture opened in July 1957, to rave reviews. There were Oscar nominations, big box office, lots of publicity. Me? I got mixed reviews, but in Norma Shearer's eyes I had become her legendary husband.

"You *are* Irving. Onscreen as well as in person. I never told you this, but *Man of a Thousand Faces* was just your audition. Now, for the first time I feel comfortable taking on *The Last Tycoon* as a film—even without a third act. I have hundreds of pages, and nowhere to go but the big screen. I'm going to call Selznick. He and I have talked about this for years. I can't wait for you to meet him."

How well I remember walking into the great David O. Selznick's office at Twentieth Century Fox! He was cordial, enthusiastic about my future, and very interested in my thoughts on Thalberg's idiosyncratic behavior. As I left his office, I said to myself, *I'm in!*

Wrong. I was out.

Selznick called Norma Shearer. "He's a nice young man, and he was adequate to play Irving opposite Jimmy Cagney. But Irving is the central character in *The Last Tycoon*, and to have the picture depend on this young man would be imprudent, both professionally and personally. We've discussed this project for too long for me not to advise you that this young man is no Irving Thalberg. To put it bluntly, Norma, the kid just doesn't have the chops. If your heart is set on him being Irving, then I'll have to bow out as producer."

Selznick was right, I didn't have the chops. But within a decade I was head of worldwide production at Paramount—and *The Last Tycoon* was on our slate. Instead of playing Irving Thalberg, I cast him in the person of Bobby De Niro, who played the part of Monroe Stahr flawlessly.

De Niro? He had the chops.

• • •

Despite his rejection, I continued to look up to David O. Selznick. He was, and always will be, the producer's producer. It was easy to understand why the producer's award was named after him.

Rejection breeds obsession. Underneath it all, I suppose I wanted to be David Selznick. When he died in 1965, the first thing I did was try to buy his home from his wife, Jennifer Jones. But it was too late. Ted Ashley, head of Warner Brothers, got there ahead of me. I didn't get the part and I didn't get the house.

Still, the Thalberg Award and the Selznick Award loomed as the Holy Grails of my profession. The two most important awards for a producer/filmmaker are both lifetime achievement awards. There's a damned good reason for that. To achieve over a long period of time in Hollywood is a matter of brains, balls, resilience, and mucho fuckin' luck. Many are called, but few are chosen. Very few have ever received the Irving Thalberg or the David O. Selznick Lifetime Achievement Awards. I wanted them both.

One day in 1980, Howard Koch, my good friend and the president of the Academy of Motion Picture Arts and Sciences, burst in unannounced.

"I've got good news. No, great news. No, *deserving* news."

Howard was a horse breeder. "I won the trifecta, huh?"

"No. I'm going to tell you a secret. Can't tell anyone. We voted last night. You've been selected to receive the Irving Thalberg Award."

"Are you putting me on?"

"No, the Academy is. They're putting you on a pedestal you deserve. I nominated you for the third time. This time, you got two shy of a unanimous vote. In other words, you beat the odds. I'm very happy for you."

He laughed.

"We're gonna do a first. We're going to toast you as a crowning example of *life imitates art*. You are the only man who played Irving Thalberg on the screen and duplicated his role in life. We're going to introduce you using the scene with you and Jimmy Cagney, and bringing you onto the stage as today's Thalberg. It'll make terrific theater, huh?"

He must have sensed something was wrong. "Smile, will ya? You're only going to make history."

I couldn't. I was too stunned. My wildest dream had come true.

It didn't last long. Two months later, I was arrested for cocaine possession. Good-bye Irving, hello infamy. Suddenly, I went from lion to lizard. Forget the Irving Thalberg Award, I became all but unemployable.

The horrific thing about this phase of my life was, I was innocent of the charge. Guilty of usage, yes, but I was three thousand miles away when the arrest went down. The fact that I had nothing whatever to do with the crime in question didn't matter, as I was to discover. I was on a roller coaster that wouldn't stop for years.

For the record, I was totally exonerated. All charges against me were dismissed, my record completely expunged.

None of that mattered to the powers that be. They couldn't get away fast enough.

Royalty fades, infamy stays.

At the time, Michael Eisner was head of Paramount. In what was described as a "carefully worded statement," he announced: "Bob is not an employee of Paramount and has not been an employee of Paramount for four years. We have a relationship with him as a producer, and nothing that has happened has changed that relationship. Paramount does not condone what he did, nor does it harshly deal with something that has no bearing on his professional relationships."

Mind you, I was innocent. It didn't matter.

How did it happen? An ambitious district attorney in Manhattan named John Martin understood that the ink I would generate for him—regardless of the worthiness of his case—could catapult him into higher political office, perhaps all the way to U.S. attorney general. For this reason and this reason alone, my name continued to be leaked to the press as a "person of interest" or a "witness." That's all the tabloids needed to generate headlines—which were the only parts of this story most people ever bothered to read.

For the next ten years, my career express-trained south, trailing headlines all the way. All of them bad. My life was consumed. And *consumed* is the word.

The best way to describe my career? The bottom line. In 1979 I was worth $11 million. A decade later? Thirty-seven bucks and falling.

Despite my exoneration, the scandal made me radioactive in Hollywood. I came to realize that a lot of things were settled in this way. A public figure is brought before the court of public opinion—a court that needs abide by zero rules of any kind before reaching a verdict. A little timely name-dropping here, some quiet "anonymous" innuendo there, and presto, you've got one cooked goose. And I had headlines, not innuendoes.

The MO? Patronizing smiles and sympathy to my face, but no return calls. After making picture after picture, I couldn't even secure a development deal. To my face? Endless praise. Behind my back? The knives were out. By law I didn't get arrested, but conversely, in my profession I *couldn't* get arrested. It ain't a good feeling going from fame to failure. And I was wearing failure with a capital *F*.

The Thalberg Award? Not to be, at least in this lifetime.

I have lived a cavalier life since before I was old enough to shave. I'm the first to admit it—I've never lived by the rules. The people who make them don't, so why should I? But when you're in the public eye, it's double-jeopardy time. You're guilty until proven innocent. And once branded, you're branded for good.

One way or another, I've been involved in the making of three hundred odd films. But none of them did for me what one book did. The reason I wrote *The Kid Stays in the Picture* was to show my son who his old man really is. He lived through this whole horrible period with me, helping me to face what I had to face. Without him to remind me of the importance of legacy, I could have easily slipped into obscurity, once and for all.

Whatever happened in my life, I was proud of what I'd accomplished. But never did I expect that an autobiography I'd written for my son would catapult me into new fame. A new generation of young people believed in the irreverent, and they responded to the book beyond anyone's expectations.

By 2000, I was more of a celebrity from the book and its audio

version than I'd ever been as a filmmaker. I couldn't go to restaurants without receiving the congratulations and adulation of
young filmmakers, audiences, and fans—a group younger than
any I had encountered since the sixties. I had touched a new
generation. Royalty I wasn't, but infamy can be more intoxicating than royalty, and certainly more dangerous. One is born into
royalty; infamy is self-made.

Walking through the gates of Paramount in 1950, a young,
razorless, pretty-boy actor under contract to the studio, I was
one step away from touchin' Heaven. Everything looked different, smelled different, tasted different. Through the eyes of a
wannabe, the City of Angels was just that: Was I dreamin' it?
Yes and no.

Now, fifty years later, I was walking up to the podium, on
the occasion of receiving my star on the Hollywood Walk of
Fame. My real estate was prime, adjacent to my dear friend,
Jack Nicholson, near the entrance to what was then Mann's Chinese Theatre. Johnny Grant, master of ceremonies and mayor
of Hollywood, introduced me to a crowd that flooded out into
the streets of Hollywood Boulevard. Them fifty years were part
dream, part nightmare. I stood to address my friends and fans,
battle-scarred from heartbreaks, yet buoyant from victories.
Amid the throng were Sumner Redstone, Sherry Lansing, Billy
Friedkin, Slash, Kate Hudson, Matthew McConaughey, Val
Kilmer, Cheryl Tiegs, Beverly Johnson, Darryl Hannah, Kelly
Lynch, and my son, Joshua, and his mother, Ali MacGraw. Mark
Wahlberg and David O. Russell addressed the crowd. Of the
nearly two hundred attendees, most had played a part in my
climb up the balsa-wood ladder.

After the ceremony, David Russell embraced me.

"Hey, Bob—that guy Wahlberg, on the podium with you just then? In a few years, we'll both be working for him." As usual, David was right.

The whole occasion was nearly hallucinogenic for me. But how perfectly I remember it. With my star in place, I was high on what seemed like my fifth life—and it wasn't over yet.

Twenty-some years after producer Howard Koch had walked into my office, dejected at having to break the news that my infamy was preventing me from receiving the Thalberg Award, a moment of déjà vu: His son Hawk, president of the Producers Guild, burst into the very same office—but this time the message was different.

"Bob, I've got news. The Producers Guild voted unanimously last night to give you the David O. Selznick Award."

Again, I was stunned. For more than twenty years I had given this up as a fantasy. I had resigned myself to the fact that infamy does not open doors to prestige. Apparently, I was wrong.

For the second time in my life, I was speechless.

"We're going to have Dustin Hoffman present you the award. He can't wait."

I hadn't spoken to Dustin in years. I was glad I was sitting down; I don't think my legs could have held me up at that point.

Could this be possible? Too much had happened for me to take this on faith. I started to count down the days till the ceremony.

On the day of the award, I was in knots. What would Hoffman say? How would I be received? I sat in the audience as impassively as I could, terrified that somehow this too would be taken away from me. As Dustin went up to the podium I realized that I was holding my breath.

Hawk Koch had told me that Dustin wasn't making a prepared speech, just presenting the award. I was expecting him simply to announce my name, call me to the stage, and that would be that. After years we'd spent at arm's length from each other, it would have been more than enough to reconcile us—and more than enough to make me feel that everything I'd been through had been more than worth it.

What happened next was so astonishing that I don't dare paraphrase it. I reproduce it here in full.

Dustin goes on stage and opens a sheaf of papers.

In a way, I probably met Robert Evans before I ever met him. At age eleven, Mr. Evans started his illustrious career on the Let's Pretend *radio show, which I listened to every Saturday morning. We were destined to work together; even then we had the same taste. But it wasn't until* Marathon Man *that I met Bob formally, and now I can thank him publicly for lobbying for me; for Sir Laurence Olivier, when no insurance company would insure him because of his illness; and for the creative and courageous choice of Marthe Keller, who could not speak one word of English except for phonetically learned lines when I met her for her screen test; and for bringing John Schlesinger, the irreplaceable Conrad Hall, and William Goldman's script, as well as Bob Towne, the finest writer of his generation, to write a critical scene, to the mix. Robert Evans pro-*

duced Marathon Man *in the fullest sense of the word.*

(Applause.)

I never met a producer like Bob before; I never met a producer like Bob, period.

(Laughter.)

To know him and to work with him is to understand the engine that put Chinatown, Rosemary's Baby, Love Story, The Godfather I *and* II, *and other films up there on the screen and beyond, into film history. Relentless, pathologically enthusiastic, not unlike Willy Loman. As Arthur Miller put it, "He's out there on a smile and a shoeshine. A salesman's got a dream, it comes with the territory."*

One day, in the middle of a tough scene on Marathon Man, *Bob approached me in between setups and in his characteristic stage whisper said, "I gotta talk to you." Motioning me to a darkened backstage area, he held out an eight-by-ten envelope that he previously held behind his back. And the following scene is forever imprinted.*

(Breaking into his legendary impersonation of me.)

He said, "You see this, you see what I have?"

"Yes, it's a script."

"No, no, no, it's not just a script." And, raising his eyebrows: "This is the finest script I've read in ten years, maybe fifteen, and you're the first to get it, okay?"

"Really?"

"I swear to God, you're the first. Not Warren, not Jack. You're the first, okay? 'Cause I want you to have it, Star."

Bob liked to call the stars he worked with "Star." And when he said it, you felt like you'd earned it.

I said, "Thank you. Thanks."

"You gotta read it tonight, as soon as you get home, okay, Star?"

I said, "I can't read it tonight, Bob, I've got so many lines to learn for tomorrow's scene, just give me a couple of days."

"I-i-i-impossible! I can't. I can't wait. You know why? Because you're the first. Not Jack, not Warren. They're gonna hear about it. It'll be very embarrassing to me. I need you to read it tonight and you gotta get back to me tomorrow. Okay, Star?"

"I can't."

"Tonight. It's important. You don't know how important this is. It's for your career. I'll be honest with you, it's for my career. This is gonna be very big. For both of us."

He pointed his finger at me and I said, "I know. I'm the first."

"You betcha. I'll see you on the set tomorrow, my boy." And as he leaves, with a wink and a smile, "You're gonna thank me, Star."

The next day, as promised, Bob was back. He patiently waited for me to finish a setup. I walked over to him.

"Did you read it?"

"Yeah, yeah, I did."

"You're the first to read it, you know that."

"I know, you told me."

"It's terrific, isn't it? I told you, it's the best script I've

read in ten years. I've never had readers' reports like it. It's a home run. We'll have our pick of directors. What do you think?"

"Well, it didn't get to me, Bob. I didn't respond to it."

"Why not?"

"Well, I don't think it works. I think it's a bad script."

"You know what? You're absolutely right. (Laughter, applause.) It's a very bad script and you're gonna make it a good script. You're gonna fix it. We're both gonna fix it. Just remember I gave it to you first. We're gonna fix it, and it's gonna be terrific, it's gonna be a home run."

That's a true story.

I don't remember the name of the script, I don't know if it got made or not. It doesn't matter. What does matter is that this was the same engine, the same enthusiasm, that gave birth to all those films you just saw up there on the screen. A producer's got a dream, it comes with the territory. Bob Evans is simply a man of dreams, a man of heart, a man of passion, a man who loves films, as much if not more than anyone in this room.

In his notes on Death of a Salesman, *Arthur Miller said that his play came from images: "The image of aging, and so many of your friends already gone, and strangers in the seats of the mighty, who do not know you, or your triumphs, or your incredible value. Above all, perhaps, the image of a need greater than hunger or sex or thirst, a need to leave a thumb print some-where on the world. The need for immortality, and by admitting it, the knowing that one has carefully in-*

scribed one's name on a cake of ice on a hot July day."

Bob understands this irony. He has always understood it. It's what makes him Bob.

In his notes to himself, about himself, in his book Bob said, "Where is everyone? Dead? Mostly. Wealthy? Some. Destitute? Many. Retired? Uh, supposedly, I ain't seen 'em. One thing I do know: I ain't dead, I ain't wealthy, I ain't destitute, and I ain't retired."

(A long silence.)

It is with deep pleasure that I present the 2003 David O. Selznick Lifetime Achievement Award to the Kid who stayed in the picture, Robert Evans.

A shock. The entire audience—close to one thousand of my peers—stood up and applauded. I began to tremble. This standing ovation? For Kid Notorious? I didn't think I'd make it to the stage. Arms embraced me. Kisses, too.

It seemed to take forever to make my way to the stage. I had to stop several times, to consciously stop the tears.

Dustin walked toward me. We embraced. To me, it was the most emotional embrace of my entire career. The picture of that magic moment will remain with me forever.

Dustin moved to the side, looking directly at me, listening intently. The crowd was applauding and still standing. It felt like hours, but it was only minutes before everyone sat and the ballroom was silent.

"It's a very tough act to follow Dustin Hoffman," I finally said. "True, isn't it, Dustin?

"You know, looking at the people here tonight, there are so

many who deserve this award more than myself. But truth's truth. I stand alone in the history of Hollywood as the only man who started his career as head of a studio and ended it as an animated cartoon." *(Laughter, applause.)*

"Many've said that David O. Selznick died broke. He didn't die broke. Maybe in dollars, but he was the richest man in this whole industry. What greater wealth is there than to be remembered through all eternity? Do me a favor, David. If I ever see you, accept me for what I am, I ain't a bad guy.

"There was only one David O. Selznick. How proud I am to get this award.

"Thank you. Thank you very much."

And I walked off the stage.

EPILOGUE

Year: 2013

It was a cold night in February—the fourteenth, to be exact. Valentine's Day.

Me, I was alone watching television. The clock had just struck eleven.

My eyes were heavy with sleep. It was dark in the room, except for the eerie glow of the large plasma television across from my bed.

Desperate to sleep off the lonely night, I ingested my best sleeping concoction—two Ambiens—and put on an old Jimmy Cagney flick, *White Heat*. A perfect mix: I passed out before Cagney went on his rant.

Hours must have passed. Then, in the distance, I heard a

voice . . . Ava Gardner's voice, interrupted by Tyrone Power, then by Errol Flynn—and by my voice in Spanish interrupting them all. I was Ambien'd out . . . or so I thought. One thing for sure: I was mesmerized. Where the hell was I?

Them Ambiens can distort the old cerebrum, but good.

What followed was akin to an LSD trip. Ava reappeared. This time she was seducing a young bullfighter: *me*! I opened my eyes, looked at the plasma screen, which was the only light in the room. Was I hallucinating? Were they really here?

Was I dead?

I closed my eyes, but the voices remained. A soft woman's touch—Ava's hands. My eyes fluttered open. Ava Gardner *was* seducing me!

"Go for it, Kid," said the long-horned director, Henry King.

I did.

My heart pounding, I staggered from the bed. Was I dreaming? No, it all happened—on the screen, that is, in the spring of 1957. Tyrone Power, Ava Gardner, Errol Flynn, Darryl Zanuck; the man himself, Ernest Hemingway; even a young punk, me. All of us in Morelia, Mexico, bringing *The Sun Also Rises* to the screen.

And then it hit me: All the cast, and even the crew, were gone. I was the only one left.

Did the Fat Lady sing? Don't know. Don't wanna. What I do know is that life is a ticket to the greatest show on earth. . . . And me?

I'm still sitting in a front-row seat.

ACKNOWLEDGMENTS

There are so many people I both need and want to thank, who have kept me alive these past few years, enabling me to finish *The Fat Lady* before she finished her song.

My thanks to Ali MacGraw, a total original. Always the giver, never the taker, and I speak with authority—forty years' worth. During my darkest hours and happiest moments, she has been there. Together we have but one child, Joshua. Why have another when you hit the jackpot the first time out? Though we have been divorced for almost half a century, our friendship has become ironclad. Ironically, Joshua, Ali, and I make a powerful family. Yes, we have been blessed big-time by the guy upstairs.

To Dickie Van Patten, my oldest friend, who to this day remains the encyclopedia of our all-but-impossible teens. We witnessed each other's misbehavior, and telling the truth about our indiscretions isn't easy for either of us. Wow, was I lucky to have a coconspirator of such dimension!

What a lucky day it was when Eric George introduced me to my literary agent, Helen Breitwieser, whose passion for this project gave me a new momentum. With her vast knowledge of the publishing industry, she introduced me to my editor, publisher Cal Morgan, and guided me throughout this process. Cal's input brought a new clarity to the book. I am truly indebted to both Helen and Cal for all of their work. Their focus and enthusiasm have culminated in ensuring that *The Fat Lady Sang* shatters new barriers in digital publishing. I would also like to thank Kathleen Baumer for all of her help and support.

For securing my safety in a litigious world, I thank the insightful Henry Holmes. For his advice and counsel, I thank my debonair friend, the erudite Eric George, who is constantly saving me from the mischievous machinations of the malevolent. A very great thanks to my dear friend Bob Shapiro, without whom my life's trek might have been cut short decades ago.

I am lucky to have survived the aforementioned challenges thanks to a brilliant team of physicians. My gratitude to my doctor Charles Kivowitz, for his careful vigilance and guidance, and not least for the understanding that he shows his impatient patient.

A heartfelt thanks to my cardiologist Robert Siegel, whose insight and skill have saved me more than once. Robert and Theresa's presence in my life continues a treasured friendship with the Siegel family.

The irrepressible and prophetic David Agus is, despite my best efforts, steadily imbuing me with a newfound optimism.

My trainer, Dion Jackson, keeps both my body and spirits in trim shape.

I want to express my gratitude to my household, a team that has supported me and shared the highs and lows for twenty years or more. First to my executive assistant and confidante Michael Binns-

Alfred, my rock, whose protective embrace and keen judgment of people, over these twenty-seven years, has yet to be found wanting. She has become part of Family Evans. To my housekeeper Rosie Chavez, who would "by any other name" still be as sweet. To the youthful Alex "Rio" Bier, who has assisted me with our extensive archive and brings his knowledge of modern communications to the battle, and to Natalia Ravanales, the latest but by no means the least member of my team.

Darryl Goldman, who started as my tennis coach, has proven himself a treasured friend these past twenty years. He is one of the family.

Dan Ramsey's skills of illumination have given Woodland its magic glow for the past twenty-five years.

At Paramount, my indispensable "Man for All Seasons," Jay Sikura, keeps the Evans banner flying.

To Ryan Rayston and Toby Burwell, who were my right and left hands in developing the structure of my bumpy ride. And to Hernan De Elejalde, who succeeded them, giving so generously of his time and skill.

I am indebted to the singular talent of my friend Michel Comte, who not only created the image but also, along with Jens Remes, designed the cover of this book. For more than a decade, Michel has put his visual insights at my disposal.

Melissa Prophet, a dynamite lady, who—separating rumor from reality—was there for me in the most dire of times. She has recently opened up the marvels of the online world and guided me into the ether.

In conclusion, I would like to thank Alan Selka, who is not only my butler, "English," but also my day-to-day brother in arms. Without his affection and creative collaboration, I could not have finished this book.

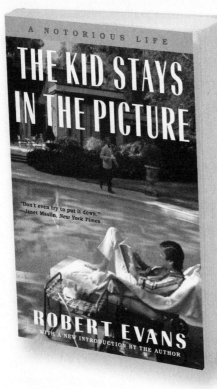